The View from
On the Road

The View from
On the
Road

The Rhetorical Vision of
Jack Kerouac

Omar Swartz

Southern Illinois University Press
Carbondale and Edwardsville

04 03 02 01   4 3 2 1

Library of Congress Cataloging-in-Publication Data
Swartz, Omar.
    The view from On the road : the rhetorical vision of Jack Kerouac /
Omar Swartz.
      p. cm.
    Includes bibliographical references and index.

    1. Kerouac, Jack, 1922–1969—Criticism and interpretation. 2. Lit-
erature and anthropology—United States—History—20th century. 3.
Kerouac, Jack, 1922–1969. On the road. 4. Conduct of life in literature. 5. Fantasy in literature. 6. Visions in literature. 7. Narration
(Rhetoric) 8. Beat generation. I. Title.
    PS3521.E7350537 1999
    813'.54—dc21   98-47092
    ISBN 0-8093-2256-0 (alk. paper)   CIP
    ISBN 0-8093-2384-2 (pbk. : alk. paper)

The paper used in this publication meets the minimum requirements of
American National Standard for Information Sciences—Permanence of
Paper for Printed Library Materials, ANSI Z39.48-1984. ∞

Again, for Rui Zhao—
A third book by which to honor you

And for my son, Avi Zhao Swartz—
Find in literature the strength and wisdom
needed to live your life well

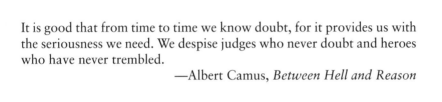

It is good that from time to time we know doubt, for it provides us with the seriousness we need. We despise judges who never doubt and heroes who have never trembled.

—Albert Camus, *Between Hell and Reason*

Contents

Preface

Jack Kerouac was a colorful figure who lived an intense and destructive life. The warmth of his fire, while it consumed him, cheers us by keeping the cold and the dark at bay. We are a nation of voyeurs—we like to watch (often from a safe distance) our idols, our heroes, and our messiahs live on the verge of an insanity and chaos that we ourselves are afraid to court.

This book argues that *On the Road* is a rhetorical document with persuasive significance in helping people to restructure their lives. The rhetorical significance of *On the Road* demands elaboration for what it can suggest about the future. Rhetoric, after all, is the study of potentialities, of changes, of futures. Kerouac's writing serves as a tool that empowers people to take control of their lives and to reject the dominant forces that constrain their thoughts and actions. Thus, the study of Kerouac is a study of rhetorical transformations.

In celebrating the margins of experience and the intensity of life, Kerouac helped develop the commitment and attitude of a larger American culture that was beginning to struggle with the tensions and contradictions of society. Through the aid of a focused narrative that graphically names and illustrates these tensions and contradictions, the reader of Kerouac's book becomes capable of responding to the larger, confusing culture in a strategic manner. Kerouac's rhetorical vision of an alternative social and cultural reality contributes to the identity of localized cultures within the United States.

Chapters 1 through 4 offer a rationale for this study, in which the relationships among Kerouac, rhetoric, and culture are highlighted. They provide biographical and historical context for readers unfamiliar with Kerouac, the "Beat Generation," or the cultural milieu of American society in the 1950s and 1960s.

Chapters 5 through 7 take the reader through the world as seen from Kerouac's writing. In particular, I explore how three visions—the Vision of Social Deviance, the Vision of Sexuality, and Dean as Vision—are dominant themes supporting Kerouac's rhetorical stance. These three visions form a clear articulation of the Beat Generation's collected fantasies and project this image onto a popular front for stronger group identification. Central to these three visions is a master analogy that pivots around the character Dean Moriarty as the "holy goof," a Christlike figure who attempts to lead the people from the cultural restraints of post–World War II America to a modified age marked by artistic, sexual, and experiential freedoms. Within Dean, an example of a new consciousness and spirituality is promoted and canonized by Kerouac.

Chapter 8 concludes with the concept of liminality. Drawing on the work of anthropologist Victor Turner and literary critic Gustavo Perez Firmat, this chapter explores how Kerouac, through his fiction, bridges and mediates the differences between his personal and liminal experiences of the world and the larger reality found in the dominant culture around him. For this study, the understanding of liminality represents the culmination of a journey to the source of perception found in Kerouac's rhetorical vision. The liminal experience provides Kerouac with the background opinions and perceptions that inform his writing.

This book owes its competency and form to Don Abbott, Ellen Abrams, Chris Bachelder, Rose Forster, Edward Schiappa, Sue Swartz, and Rui Zhao. In one way or another, each of these people played an instrumental role in my ability to complete this project.

Sections of this book have appeared in other forums. Part of chapter 1 appeared as "Rhetorical Transformation in Kerouac's *On the Road*," *Communication and Theater Association of Minnesota* 24 (1997): 35–49. Part of chapter 8 appeared as "A Liminal View of *On the Road*," *Speech and Theater Association of Missouri Journal* 27 (1997): 56–64. I am grateful for permission to reproduce the material here.

Part One
Departures

1

Rhetorical
Transformations

Jack Kerouac is an American author who, to this day, is often misunderstood by his critics and idolized by his followers. In ancient Greece, Kerouac would have been honored as a rhapsode, a wandering poet who embodied the wisdom of his era (Enos 1978). Yet in the mid-twentieth-century America that Kerouac celebrates and exalts as Walt Whitman did one hundred years earlier, Kerouac remains something of an enigma. In holding up a mirror to the culture of his time, Kerouac enabled others to grow excited by what they saw and agitated at what he implied. In a culture that often kills its messiahs (Mencken 1994), Kerouac lived and died by evoking his supporters—who subsequently caged him and turned him into an icon—and by provoking oppositional pressures. Ultimately, Kerouac died a martyr's death. Willingly or unwillingly, he became a cultural "hero" who gave a spirit to an age and an identity to those resisters who struggled against the forces of conformity.

Kerouac spent his adult life chronicling his existence through thinly veiled autobiographical novels, and he shared with his audience the trials and exultations of his experience. Such behavior was hardly unusual for a young author growing up in twentieth-century America. J. D. Salinger, Norman Mailer, Kurt Vonnegut, and scores of other writers were all similarly engaged in documenting their lives. Yet Kerouac is somehow different from his literary contemporaries; his writing does more than merely contribute to the bulk of American letters. This "more" needs to be contextualized. For instance, many writers produced better prose and are more celebrated for their art; they can be found canonized in our university English departments. Yet, Kerouac is both an icon and an iconoclast. Until recently, he was not appreciated by university literature professors. Kerouac and his fellow "Beat" writers have existed for decades on the fringes of academic scholarship and institutional respectability.

In spite of such neglect and the fact that most of his novels never sold well, Kerouac accomplished something that most writers aspire to but few achieve. Through the careful documentation of his own existence and thought and with his critical eye toward tensions and potentialities in American culture, Kerouac was able to make a significant mark on our society and to help modify in fundamental ways important aspects of the national psyche. Kerouac redrew many of the cultural maps upon which American intellectual and social terrain is situated, and he instigated a revolution in consciousness. This consciousness, understood broadly as a humanizing and rebellious attitude, peaked in the turbulent 1960s but remains today an important, though lesser, force in American society.

This book argues that Kerouac's influence on American society is largely rhetorical. His significance as a cultural icon can best be understood in terms of traditional rhetorical practices and principles. Kerouac must be seen as a rhetor who symbolically reconstructs his world and offers arguments and encouragements for others to follow. I offer an explanation for Kerouac's influence by elucidating the rhetorical dimensions of *On the Road*. More specifically, this study proposes that *On the Road* constitutes a "rhetorical vision." Rhetorical visions are large meta-narratives (reality-defining discourses), encapsulated ideologies, prophetic inquiries that suggest alternative possibilities for growth and change. They are symbolically situated desires that have the power to transform images of self, society, and others. Rhetorical visions unify diversity, unite fragmentation, and transcend the individual to enact a new rationality. They serve a paradigmatic function in establishing the boundaries of a person's world.[1] In the West, the archetypical rhetorical vision is Christianity. The Bible offers a series of large narratives that symbolically restructure people's relationships with themselves and the world (Burke 1970).

The impetus for a detailed examination of the rhetorical implications of Kerouac's role in influencing American society comes from a statement made by John Clellon Holmes, Beat novelist and friend of Kerouac, reflecting on the excitement of the 1960s: "[A] new vision is abroad in the land, a vision that was fathered by my generation's attitudes and antics, a vision that perhaps can be best understood by understanding us" (1967, 12). Holmes argues that in order to understand the changes that were taking place in the 1960s, scholars must first understand the people of his generation, specifically the core group of artists and bohemians known as the "Beats." The Beats, as John Tytell writes, "[W]ere the creative souls of the fifties" (1976, 30). Arguably, Kerouac was the central visionary and spokesperson of this group that numbered in its ranks cultural luminaries such as William S. Burroughs, Lawrence Ferlinghetti, Allen Ginsberg, Michael McClure, Amiri Baraka/Leroi Jones, and Gary Snyder. Kerouac's vision was instrumental in articulating the group's consciousness and in giving it thematic unity. Extending beyond this group, Kerouac's *On the Road* projects the primary vision for what in the late 1950s and early 1960s promised to be a "new age."

In order to develop the thesis that *On the Road* is a rhetorical document with persuasive significance in helping people to restructure their lives, I offer a "fantasy theme analysis," a method that a reader can use to understand the cultural dimensions of a text. Because rhetorical visions involve large, encompassing (and sometimes unwieldy) narratives, a fantasy theme analysis is a localized way to establish "meaning" in a text. Thus, fantasy theme analysis presents the structure of a rhetorical vision in a digestible fashion. Rhetorical critics, in particular, use fantasy theme analysis to make connections between texts and the rhetorical efforts of their authors.

From the vantage point of the late twentieth century, a discussion of Kerouac and a celebration of his rhetorical influence may seem anachronistic. The promises and the potentials of the 1960s counterculture have been shattered by reactionary forces, especially those of the "Reagan Era," and the rise in power of the GOP. Repression and authoritarianism is everywhere on the rise, both in this country and throughout the world, and new political policies, exemplified in the GOP's "Contract with America," perpetuate a stultifying social order. Many gains the Left has made since its late-1960s political heyday have steadily eroded. Accentuating the problem, as Ernesto Laclau and Chantal Mouffe explain, is the fact that the social analysis of Left politics is less sure of itself and its monumental task:

> Left-wing thought today stands at a crossroads. The "evident truths"
> of the past—the classical forms of analysis and political calculation,
> the nature of the forces in conflict, the very meaning of the Left's
> struggles and objectives—have been seriously challenged by an ava-
> lanche of historical mutations which have riven the ground on which
> those truths were constituted. (1985, 1)

Why, then, study Kerouac and his vision, a vision antithetical to the dominant values that currently control our nation? Why struggle for plurality, change, and multivocality in a political climate that increasingly champions a monolithic silence? The answer is that Kerouac *deserves* further study. Specifically, the rhetorical significance of *On the Road* demands elaboration for what it can suggest about the future. Rhetoric, after all, is the study of potentialities, of changes, of futures (Poulakos 1984). This work, therefore, is intended as an act of resistance. It is an attempt to subvert the dominant political paradigm by illustrating the transformational powers of rhetoric. Scholarship and criticism are acts intended to influence the future and to have social impact (Swartz 1997). As the world grows more conservative and as American leadership and culture play an instrumental part in promoting what has been called a "fascist" social, cultural, and political consciousness (Gross 1980), individual acts of resistance, particularly those that attempt to revive alternative spaces upon which to construct identity, are necessary. Kerouac's writing serves as a tool that empowers people to take control of their lives and to reject the dominant forces that constrain their thoughts and their actions. Thus, this study of Kerouac is a study of rhetorical transformation.[2]

Naming as Rhetorical Action

Writers, speakers, and poets have always been persuaders; they use language to articulate visions and to reinforce social realities. From the ancient rhapsodes on, the mythic-poetic episteme has played a dialectical role with logos in the functioning of Western culture. While the norms of myths and poetry change over the years, and while new epistemologies may rise in time to challenge the supremacy of old poetic norms, the fact remains that human knowledge is largely based in language, metaphor, and narrative (see Burke 1969a; Foucault 1970; Whorf 1956; and White 1987). On a less philosophical level, the relationship between a writer and his or her rhetorical intent is often overt and explicit. As William Burroughs explains, novelists attempt to change the world with their work:

> [Writers] are trying to create a universe in which they have lived or would like to live. . . . Sometimes, as in the case of Fitzgerald and Kerouac, the effect produced by a writer is immediate, as if a generation were waiting to be written. (qtd. in Clark 1984, "Epigraph")

Do writers write generations? In a sense, they do. "Generations" are rhetorical constructs, identifications that people make with symbols. To name a generation involves localizing reality and limiting its experience to a particular politics for a particular group of people. In other words, people join generations, they are not born into them, and these affiliations are based partly upon experience but mostly on the internalization of a collection of symbols, fantasies, biases, and ideologies (McGee 1975).

Within any single generation, there has to be some unifying theme. Thus, we can speak of generation "gaps" or of people belonging to generations to which their age does not chronologically correspond. Generations are thematic and have a resonant voice or vision that unifies the people who claim membership.

Kerouac's lightning-bolt influence in American culture is indicative of a vision with a high cultural resonance. The phrase "cultural resonance" is another way of saying that a vision has meaning within the context of a group of people who subscribe to similar beliefs, values, or judgments. Visions function as rhetorical phenomena because they speak *to*, as well as *from*, a certain audience. By "rhetorical," I suggest that Kerouac's vision is a strategic argument that negotiates between competing world-views, creating new alternatives.

Rhetoric, as defined in this book, means a system or strategy of meanings and/or negotiations, embodied in argument or narrative, that invites participation and expansion. Rhetoric is an invitation to *be* something. People are born onto the planet but are placed into the world. This act of placement is a form of becoming: rhetoric is the opportunity to actualize this transformation. The condition of rhetoric, therefore, involves the ultimate democratic experience, for it offers a perspective, gives reasons for it, and encourages individual participation and expansion. Society is the expression of a collective rhetorical will; within society, a rhetorical vision is a specific instance of a communal construction of social reality. Rhetorical visions differ from other visions by building upon a prevalent shared network of group fantasies, projections of an ideal world, a world that can become; a community then projects this image onto a popular front for stronger group identification. The stronger the group identification, the more "real" reality becomes for that group. Correspondingly, the stakes also rise. "Culture wars," which can be conceptualized as conflicts between competing rhetorical visions, are accentuated by higher spiritual and material antes.

Rhetorical visions, comprised of fantasy themes—codes for identification and persuasion—were originally discussed by Ernest G. Bormann. In his 1972 essay, Bormann discusses how groups of people coalesce around in-group dramas that serve as repertoires for group identification and meaning. Within groups, people signify. These significations establish the parameters within which understanding can occur. Signification occurs as the result of dramas that aggregate to form extended narratives. To the extent that these dramas involve large groups of people, their "meanings" become "reality," a symbolic reality. The narrative that gives structure to this meaning is what Bormann calls a "rhetorical vision" (398). The rhetorical vision, in short, is constructed of fantasy themes that extend throughout the group, creating a group culture. As this group grows in size and significance, as it gains public and widespread acceptance, it becomes a vision that competes with the dominant vision of a society. The rhetorical dimension of a vision derives from its implied confrontation with the recalcitrance of the status quo. It is not defensible to argue that a single dominant rhetorical vision existed to direct dissent among the various resistance and countercultural movements of the 1960s. However, it is feasible to argue that Kerouac's *On the Road* embodies the most mature expression of his personal vision and that it played a significant role in reweaving patches of the social fabric of this country's culture.

With the 1957 publication of *On the Road*, a vision of social revolt was named and became identified as a national movement. The naming of a revolt is often more important in giving that revolt social significance than the actual revolt itself. In American society, at least, revolt is often dialectical—few movements, if any, have overturned American society. What becomes important in any communication study of American social movements is not just the fact that people revolted, but that they were able to publicly *name* their discontent and to focus their energies in a rhetorical/political manner. Chronic discontent often exists in all societies, particularly those as socially/materially oppressive and racist as American society was in the 1950s and 1960s. Discontent, however, cannot metamorphose into social change unless it is directed into a particular symbolization. Discontent needs focus and discipline in order to generate change and opportunity. The act of naming is the rhetorical act of focus and discipline. As Michel Foucault explains:

> Rhetoric defines the spatiality of representation as it comes into being with language; grammar [or visions that serve as a kind of cultural grammar] defines in the case of each individual language the order that distributes that spatiality in time. This is why, as we shall see, grammar presupposes languages, even the most primitive and spontaneous ones, to be rhetorical in nature. (1970, 84)

Seen another way, social revolt, as any type of rhetorical endeavor, has to be "entitled." Rhetorical action names a situation, sums up events, and otherwise makes sense out of material reality. Human experience is a rhetorical experience that is shaped by visions or narratives and guided (or goaded) by hierarchy and ideology (Burke 1966, 359–79). As Edward Schiappa explains, "The categorizing function of language can be a form of symbolic inducement; different terminologies prompt us to perceive the world in different ways" (1992, 9; for elaboration, see Gregg 1984). Historically, *On the Road* acted as an important symbolic inducement to fuse together a diverse range of Americans. Historian Bruce Cook discusses, in nondisciplinary terms, the process of entitlement and how it relates to Kerouac:

> Perhaps it was only that the time had come at last for just such an explosion of interest and *On the Road* only supplied the necessary fuse. Or maybe this was the kind of book that spoke so directly and eloquently to the generation that was waiting for it and that it needed only to be announced to be recognized. However we account for it, there can be no doubt that it was through Jack Kerouac and his book that the general public became instantly aware of the Beat Generation. (1971, 72)

The book did more than merely make the country "aware" of the Beat Generation; it amplified and popularized the condition of knowledge that gave the signifier "Beat Generation" cultural significance and resonance. As Cook documents, *On the Road* "spoke" to Kerouac's generation. In speaking to a "generation," the text creates its audience (cf. Park 1982). But how does a text "speak"? Kerouac spoke to his generation because his text constructed, in part, that generation, as it helped construct, in part, the generation of young people in the 1960s.

The connection between the "beatniks," the countercultural followers of Kerouac in the late 1950s, and the "hippies," as they metamorphosed into, is well documented (George and Starr 1985). For instance, Ann Charters develops this theme in her biography of Kerouac. As she explains, "Twenty years after [Neal] Cassady took Kerouac on the road, a generation of rock stars epitomized their earlier search for a lifestyle beyond the conformity of middle-class America" (1973, 289). The connection between the two groups is best exemplified by Neal Cassady, who has the dual honor of being the first "Beat" as well as the first "hippie." Accentuating the importance of Cassady in the genealogy of the 1960s counterculture, Cook writes: "The presence of Neal Cassady in the Merry Pranksters offered to those who might have looked with skepticism on the group some evidence of continuity. He was a link with the genuine Beat past" (1971, 198).[3]

"Beat," Rhetorical Style, and Madness

It is not just *what* Kerouac wrote that gave the counterculture its identity, it is *how* he wrote it as well. Kerouac's theme in *On the Road* is freedom, and his writing style, which he described as "spontaneous prose," was the vehicle of this freedom's expression and vision. His approach to writing was modeled after jazz musicians. In a *Paris Review* interview, Kerouac explains the influence of jazz and "bop" in his work:

> Yes, jazz and bop, in the sense of a, say, a tenor man drawing a breath
> and blowing a phrase on his saxophone, till he runs out of breath,
> and when he does, his sentence, his statement's been made . . . that's
> how I therefore separate my sentences, as breath separations of the
> mind. (qtd. in Berrigan 1968, 83)

Style, it must remembered, is itself a substance of knowledge, a reality that argues self-consciously for its own presence in the world. As Kenneth Burke explains, style is a strategic intervention on behalf of a persuader: "These strategies size up the situations, name their structure and outstanding ingredients, and name them in a way that contains an attitude toward them" (1973, 1). This is especially true for Kerouac, whose writing style enacts a merger between content and experience. As Kerouac explains, "The prose is what I believe to be the prose of the future, from both the conscious top and the unconscious bottom of the mind, limited only by the limitations of time flying by as your mind flies by with it" (qtd. in Charters 1973, 9). According to Holmes, Kerouac's writing style was "seeking to free the whole range of his consciousness to the page—the consciousness that was one continuous, vivid flow of sense-data, associations, memories, and meditations" (1967, 81).

As spontaneous prose is the vehicle for Kerouac's vision of an experience unfettered by the demands of corporate America and the stifling conformity of the middle-class status quo, the catalyst for Kerouac's fantasy-theme alternatives is Neal Cassady, the now-legendary prototype of *On the Road*'s protagonist, Dean Moriarty. Cassady lived the life that Kerouac so carefully documented in *On the Road*, and he is testament to the revolutionary potential of a subversive social consciousness. Born in the back seat of a jalopy as his parents were traveling across the country to find work in 1926, Cassady was a man attracted to the cracks and holes of life in the modern era. Raised on the streets of Denver and in pool halls, reform schools, and libraries, Cassady rejected the fabrication of American culture by government and industry and instead pursued his own vision of life based on the joys and exultations of experience. Looking back on his writing of *On the Road*, Kerouac explained: "I wanted to give a concise poetic opinion of Neal. They used to put guys in the nut house for that [iconoclasm] in the days of Christopher Smart" (qtd. in Charters 1973, 9).

Kerouac's allusion to Christopher Smart in reference to Cassady is significant. Smart was an eighteenth-century English poet who was plagued his entire life by both debt and madness (*Directory* 1921). He twice served time in Bedlam, an infamous English madhouse. Accentuating both problems was Smart's affinity for taverns and for his art—he pursued both with such intensity, at the expense of other obligations, that he was unable to provide for his wife and children. On several occasions, Smart was arrested by his creditors. In many ways, Cassady is similar to Smart. A poet who lived rather than wrote his poetry, Cassady existed on the verge of madness. Accentuating his life's intensity were alcohol and drugs. Cassady was frequently unable to provide for his family, especially when he was in jail or prison—he served two years in San Quentin for selling two marijuana cigarettes to undercover police officers—or when he was otherwise lost to the world during his numerous national and transcontinental wanderings. For Kerouac, both Smart and Cassady represent men on the verge of experience/insanity, people who prescribe their own reality rather than digest the reality given to them by society.

While an identification between Smart and Cassady is not exact, there is, nevertheless, a sense in which the comparison of them exemplifies the core of Kerouac's vision for America. Central to Kerouac's vision is freedom. This freedom is different from the freedom celebrated in the national American mythology (Parenti 1994); Kerouac is not interested in the myths of economic or political freedom. These shallow cultural truisms are irrelevant for Kerouac; they are absent in his cultural conversation. Kerouac is not interested in traditional politics and traditional understandings of power. Rather, he is interested in a transcendental freedom, the freedom that both Smart and Cassady embody: freedom to be "mad," mad for life, hungry for experience. Kerouac's freedom breaks the bonds of marriage, family life, work, and traditional American corporate experience; it is a freedom that verges on religious ecstasy (both in the sense of Western and Eastern mysticism).

The word "beat" itself, coined by Kerouac (and by Herbert Huncke), has many connotations that relate to the above discussion. First, "beat" implies rhythm, especially the free-flowing rhythm of experimental jazz. Kerouac and the other Beats were jazz enthusiasts and frequently read their poetry to jazz accompaniment. Kerouac recorded three poetry albums, one of which is a dialectic exchange between Kerouac and two famous jazz musicians, Zoot Sims and Al Cohn.[4] Second, in the sense that it was commonly or popularly understood, the word "beat" referred to being broken, beaten down, pushed to the margins of existence by a cruel and hostile world. This sense of the word refers to people who, like Cassady or Herbert Huncke, were from the streets, petty criminals, the children of street urchins and other marginalized victims of American society. In the first public discussion of the "Beat Generation," Holmes explains this connotation of "beat":

> More than mere weariness, it implies the feeling of having been used, of being raw. It involves a sort of nakedness of mind, and ultimately, of soul; a feeling of being reduced to the bedrock of consciousness.

> In short, it means being undramatically pushed up against the wall
> of oneself. A man is beat whenever he goes for broke and wagers the
> sum of his resources on a single number and the young generation
> has done that continually from early youth. (1952, 10)

Finally, "beat," as Kerouac came to insist toward the end of his life,
represented a religious experience; it meant "beatitude," a Catholic condition of blessedness (Sorrell 1982). In an important sense, all three of
these definitions represent a similar theme: to be "beat" was to be in
another time—to be in your body physically but to be outside of the
solidarity that people generally feel for one another. The rhythm of the
drums, the desolation of the streets, the bliss of beatification—all imply
a break with normal time, a transcendent of the mundane. All three conditions lead to new perspectives of the world. To be "beat" is to force one's
self, or to be forced, to explore new forms of consciousness and being.

The temporal aspect is important to emphasize because a person's sense
of being is always associated with a particular historicity (Foucault 1977).
By taking a nonstandard approach to time, as Kerouac frequently does
in *On the Road*, in which he has hallucinations that take him back and
forth in time (confusing the present and the past), Kerouac challenges the
reification of consciousness as it is experienced by most Americans. In
an important sense, all three definitions of "beat" are conditions of
liminality—discussed more fully in chapter 8, which analyzes the liminal experience in *On the Road*.

In a famous passage from the novel, Kerouac describes the madness
that he pursued in his life, the madness he found in Neal Cassady. This
madness strikes at the core of "beat" for Kerouac; it embodies all three
notions discussed above. In particular, the passage represents Kerouac's
belief that "true" experience could not be found in the safety of conformity and middle-class values:

> I shambled after as I've been doing all my life after people who in-
> terest me, because the only people for me are the mad ones, the ones
> who are mad to live, mad to talk, mad to be saved, desirous of ev-
> erything at the same time, the ones who never yawn or say a com-
> monplace thing, but burn, burn, burn, like fabulous yellow Roman
> candles exploding like spiders across the stars and in the middle you
> see the blue centerlight pop and everybody goes "Aww!" (1957, 9)

By recognizing madness, in the form of intense desire, as a virtue, as
Gilles Deleuze and Felix Guattari would do years later when they declared
that "desire produces reality" (1983, 30), Kerouac vindicates the unrec-
ognized genius of people existing on the margin of high experience.[5] In a
sense, the "mad" ones that Kerouac worships are "anti-ego"; their sense

of self and others dissipates and they merge, schizophrenically, into the bliss of experience, as they are still tied to the world through their bodies. This experience burns with intensity and life. For a few moments these people bring to the fore the brilliance of human potential and desire that escapes commodification and commercialization. These are the geniuses who live their poetry rather than write it (Burke 1984, 74–79), the pious people who are true to the perceived "nature" of their selves,[6] the unsung artists and cultural heroes that push back the walls of human limitation and perception. These are the people who live and die to release the human being from the cages of our own construction.

In studying people like Cassady, Kerouac saw an aura of brilliance emanating from the spirits of frantic men who pressed the forms of their existence to the limits of experience. The fact that these actions were done in madness—or in other disregard for the constraints or limitations of the body—seemed only to add appeal to their calling and to legitimize the authenticity of their motives. Thus, these personalities—best exemplified in Cassady, but later in Ken Kesey and in the Grateful Dead—accumulated an almost saint-like status among their followers as holy prophets opposing the caution and conformity of post-World War II America (see Wolfe 1968).

In celebrating the margins of experience and the intensity of life, and in glorifying the struggle between the individual and the bourgeois ego that threatens to create compliant citizens in the capitalist social order, Kerouac helped develop the commitment and attitude of a larger American culture that was beginning to struggle with the tensions and contradictions of society in ways that Cassady magnified. Philosophically speaking, Kerouac's *On the Road* reveals "the split between the unity of a culture as it exists symbolically and the individual's actual fragmentary and contradictory experience of that culture" (Hunt 1981, 241). Tim Hunt's observation complements the approach to Kerouac that my study embraces: by recognizing the split, through the aid of a focused narrative that graphically names and illustrates the problem, the reader of Kerouac's book becomes capable of responding to the larger, confusing culture in a strategic manner. Kerouac's rhetorical vision of an alternative social and cultural reality contributes to the identity of localized cultures of interacting group members. These groups constantly grow and network and contribute to an awareness through which members live privately articulated narratives and stimulate in others a feeling that the world has order, structure, heroes, villains, saints, dreams, and art (Bales 1970, 152). Robert F. Bales, the psychologist who first documented the importance that fantasy plays in achieving group coherence and in influencing interpersonal behavior, explains the importance of narrative in structuring people's perceptions:

> In the fantasy of a group culture, as in a work of art, things are closer
> to the heart's desire than in the everyday world. . . . [The fantasy]
> contains images of men and women, elders and children, gods and
> devils, animals, plants, and minerals. Images of time unfold, the sea-
> sons change, and the great adversaries of destiny loom and clash.
> (152)

The recognition of the split between culture and the role of the individual enables people to participate in an alternative shared fantasy.
Kerouac's genius in *On the Road* is his ability to accentuate an alternative narrative and to localize it in the desires of many young people in
this country and throughout the world.

2

Kerouac in Context

Jack Kerouac was born in Lowell, Massachusetts, in 1922. He died in Florida in 1969 from internal hemorrhaging brought on by his alcoholism. Kerouac's working-class family was French-Canadian, raising Kerouac under the guidance of Catholicism. He studied in parochial schools where he learned to speak and read English as a second language. He had one older brother, Gerard, who died when Kerouac was a child, and a sister who died when he was much older. Kerouac was a strong, husky man with considerable athletic ability. He was recruited by Columbia University to play football, and his enrollment at that school was a decisive event in his life, for it was at Columbia that Kerouac was exposed to the excitement and lure of New York City. Within a few years he had met and befriended people such as William S. Burroughs, Lucien Carr, Hal Chase, and Allen Ginsberg. With these people, Kerouac became exposed to the men and women of the criminal underclass that he would romanticize in many of his novels.

At Columbia, Kerouac soon lost interest in football, rejecting the authority of the coach as he would reject all authority in his life. However, by losing interest in football, Kerouac lost his scholarship and subsequently was unable to remain in school. Kerouac enthusiastically departed from Columbia, using his newly freed time to read voraciously, write continuously, and intensify his experiences in the city, where he solidified his relationship with a crowd of petty criminals and drug abusers, including Ginsberg and the slightly older William Burroughs. These three men belonged to a larger collection of men and women, in major cities throughout the United States, that had an informal network of liaisons and influences. Picking up on this small but highly visible subculture in the United States, the media, using Kerouac's cue, identified it as the "Beat Generation."

In light of the media blitz that surrounded the reception of many of their works, Kerouac, Ginsberg, Burroughs, and Neal Cassady became the Beat culture's most celebrated and controversial representatives. Others, such as Ferlinghetti, Holmes, McClure, and Snyder, also contributed to a poetic cultural resurgence/resistance (Davidson 1989; Kherdian 1967). In particular, under the influence of Ferlinghetti, founder of City Lights Books, San Francisco soon replaced New York as the mecca of the new American cultural movement.[1] This is not surprising as the "West" had an aura of potentiality to it in much Beat literature. Throughout the late 1960s, northern California, in particular the Bay Area, was a popular place for people to gather from across the country in communes and communities to live out their shared visions.[2]

In the decade following his departure from Columbia, Kerouac wrote novels and rambled throughout the United States and Mexico, following his friends and getting his "kicks" where he could. His travels brought him through the armed services and marriage, neither of which kept his attention for long (he had one child whom he rejected and denied his entire life). Kerouac made a career out of being a wanderer and hobo, all the while recording his thoughts and sights in his journals. Kerouac's first book, *The Town and the City*, was published in 1950. Written in the style of Thomas Wolfe, it was not a success; it brought him little fame or financial security. More damaging to Kerouac's development as a writer, however, was the fact that publishing the book was a difficult experience. Kerouac's rejection of authority led him to oppose stringently the efforts of editors to help him publish his work. He claimed that the demands of the publishing process stifled his creativity as a writer. As a result, Kerouac cut himself off from the publishing world and wrote book after book in his own idiom, circulating the manuscripts among his friends, the growing community of yet-to-be-publicized "Beats."

The 1952 publication of Holmes's *Go* and the 1956 publication of Ginsberg's *Howl*, and the publicity from the obscenity trial that resulted from it (see Ferlinghetti 1976), created conditions in the publishing world conducive to Kerouac's books. The eventual publication and success of *On the Road* surprised Kerouac, who was very shy, and surrounded him with a notoriety that turned increasingly hostile. Overnight, Kerouac was transformed from obscurity into a star. Many of the books that Kerouac had been hoarding all the years he was on the road were published in rapid succession, as well as a few new ones.[3] However, his fantastic burst of creativity had been spent. Within a few years, the pressures of his fame and notoriety, along with his accelerated use of alcohol and drugs, exacted their toll, first on his creativity and then on his health. Kerouac died in Florida, a sick and broken man, spurned by the world and spurning the world. He died resenting the very social world that he helped create, that existed and continues to exist, in part, in his own image. It was only after he died that he was recognized for the hero that he was among the people he helped give a voice to—Bob Dylan, members of the Doors, and the Grateful Dead all paid homage to him, as did many writers, social movement leaders, and other members of the cultural Left. These people found in Kerouac the initial spark that they needed to recreate themselves and to begin their work in transforming society. As is the case of so many prophets, Kerouac died young and left to the next generation the task of developing his vision.

On the Road and the Cult of High Experience

Kerouac's experiences during the years 1946 to 1950 are recorded in two primary sources, On the Road and Visions of Cody. These so-called "road books" are thinly veiled travel diaries that chronicle the adventures and lifestyles of Sal Paradise and Dean Moriarty (also called Jack Duluoz and Cody Pomeray in other works), fictional counterparts to Jack Kerouac and Neal Cassady.[4] Kerouac traveled with Cassady, lived with Cassady, and tape-recorded their conversations in his effort to know Cassady and to understand the depths of his euphoric existence. Kerouac's relationship with Cassady may even have been sexual at times, as Kerouac, Cassady, and Ginsberg all engaged in homosexual relationships.[5] Ecstasy for these men was to a large degree phallic and associated with the Greek connections between knowledge and sperm.[6] To a large degree, women were marginalized from these men's existence and were relegated to the role of care givers or sex objects (a point evident in Johnson 1983 and Ehrenreich 1983). More will be discussed on this point in chapter 6.

While Kerouac maintained that Visions of Cody is his masterpiece, the book itself was not published in its entirety until 1972 and hence falls outside the direct parameters of this study. It nevertheless was known by reputation among the Beats and provides much of the context for a wider understanding of On the Road, the more influential and popular of the two works. Visions of Cody certainly deserves mention before beginning a journey down Kerouac's road; any understanding of Kerouac requires an understanding of his relationship with Neal Cassady, and Visions of Cody is Kerouac's personal and private testimony to the brilliantly disturbed Cassady. Moreover, both Visions of Cody and On the Road represent the clearest expression of Kerouac's "voice" as a writer. Both books were written to capture the motion and influence that was Neal Cassady. Both cover many of the same events in the young men's lives.

On the Road is a novel of experience and adventure, of impressions and expanded awareness. The book is a celebration of life and youth. *On the Road* brings youth consciousness to new heights. More than popularizing "beatness," in any of its three connotations, *On the Road* presents to a large popular audience what can be identified as the "cult of high experience." Broadly, the cult of high experience was an attitude that fermented with the Beat Generation, involving the belief that experience rather than conformity was the natural condition of the healthy human being. What followed the publication of *On the Road* was the appearance of a generation of converts who, like Kerouac and his persona, Sal Paradise, became "turned on" by Cassady's embodiment of movement and freedom and followed with their own imitations. The cult of high experience involved the loose ideology that "anything goes" and that the more intense the flame, the more valuable the fire. Rock and roll, as it was personified by people like Jim Morrison, was one cultural practice that was influenced by this cult and characterized the counterculture through the early 1970s (Riordan and Prochnicky 1991).

The cult of high experience finds its representation in Cassady, who embodies the victory of bodily desire over the limitations of societal constraints. Holmes notes that in the books featuring Cassady, Kerouac presents his most profound "portrait of the young, rootless American, high on life." Furthermore, as Holmes maintains, Kerouac clearly articulates the feeling, shared by many, "that a certain reckless idealism, a special venturesomeness of heart, had been outlawed to the margins of American life in his time" (1967, 76). Holmes elaborates:

> Kerouac expresses most clearly his vision of America . . . at once cruel and tender, petty and immense; and in [Cassady] himself, he embodies both the promise of America's oldest dream (the unbuttoned soul venturing toward a reconciliation of its contradictions) and the bitter fact of its contemporary debauching (the obscenely blinking police car that questions anyone "moving independently of gasoline"). (76)

The cult of high experience, restless and uncompromising, invites an honest appraisal of the U.S. cultural wasteland, rejects the conformity, mediocrity, and oppression of the United States, and runs on a rhetorical fuel generated by the tensions caused by the "debauching" of American potentialities. "If we are truly a free nation," maintains the cult of high experience, "then let's act like we are a free nation and let it all hang out." Unfortunately, the vast potentialities of our social landscape are policed by the representatives of hypocrisy that call into question and check the tendencies of self-expression and social independence.[7]

In *On the Road*, Sal and Dean embark on an exhausting foray that brings them through the slums of New York, Denver, San Francisco, New Orleans, Mexico, and points in between. While exploring the bohemian underworld of vice, sex, drugs, and nonconformity, the men search for new meaning in their lives. These meanings derive from lessons learned on the road, from interactions with the marginalized, the simple, the poor people they meet in their travels. Inspired by these experiences, bordering on the criminal and the insane, Kerouac (as Walt Whitman before him) describes with a religious tone all that unfolds before him as if he were simply an eyewitness of the manifest glory of God.[8] In the manifest glory of existence that Kerouac celebrates, he manages to transform the pettiness and sorrow of life in 1950s America into an expression of wonder and revelation. Kerouac secularizes his Catholicism and brings God into the level of the mundane experience of "getting by." Kerouac makes the body sacred and embodies the sacred in Cassady. An early example of Kerouac's gift for uplifting the commonplace comes as he crosses into the West for the first time, in search of Cassady:

> I woke up as the sun was reddening; and that was the one distinct time in my life, the strangest moment of all, when I didn't know who I was—I was far away from home, haunted and tired with travel, in a cheap hotel room I'd never seen, hearing the hiss of steam outside, and the creak of the old wood of the hotel, and the footsteps upstairs, and all the sad sounds, and I looked at the cracked high ceiling and really didn't know who I was for about fifteen strange seconds. I wasn't scared; I was just somebody else, some stranger, and my whole life was a haunted life, the life of a ghost. I was halfway across America, at the dividing line between the East of my youth and the West of my future. (1957, 16)

Kerouac, as represented by Sal Paradise, has been bitten by the bug of Dean's madness. In joining Dean Moriarty in his quest for experience and freedom, Sal journeys across America, ostensibly searching for Dean's missing father. Dean's lost father symbolizes, in this time of atomic threat, the loss of authority or the loss of faith that Americans had in a figure that they could turn to for guidance and comfort. This absence represents the betrayal of the average American by U.S. cultural and political institutions. Dean's father, after all, was an average citizen with a wife and child, no different from thousands of other men who fall on hard times and never manage to recover. His offspring, Dean (and by spiritual extension, Sal), uses his father's disappearance as an excuse to shirk his responsibilities to the social order and to pursue his own cultural ideal.

In the pursuit of Dean's father, which never really becomes anything more than an excuse to roam aimlessly among the bums and dispossessed, Sal and Dean reveal the more fundamental object of their journey: the relentless pursuit of "IT!" As Kerouac makes clear throughout his book, IT! signifies the indescribable moment of perfect understanding when the sensating individual and the sting of time blend indistinguishably against the "blank tranced end of all innumerable riotous angelic particulars that had been lurking in our souls all our lives" (1957, 172). IT! is an existential moment, perhaps *the* existential moment, when the truth that is locked behind the plastic and painted and artificial constraints of our identities is allowed to break through and consume consciousness. IT! is a state of religious exultation and exuberance, an expression of the orgasmic oneness and unity of creation. For Sal and Dean, IT! can be found at a spiritual apex, where the consciousness of an individual is transformed by some catalyst, usually sex or drugs or intense deprivation and despair. IT! is usually associated with some marginalized condition. For instance, while watching a musician in a night club, Dean Moriarty explains to Sal Paradise how the experience of IT! can be aroused through the medium of jazz expression:

> "All of a sudden somewhere in the middle of the chorus he *gets* it—everybody looks up and knows; they listen; he picks it up and carries. Time stops. He's filling empty space with the substance of our lives, confessions of his bellybottom strain, remembrance of ideas, rehashes of old blowing. He has to blow across bridges and come back and do it with such infinite feeling soul-exploratory for the tune of the moment that everybody knows it's not the tune that counts but IT." (1957, 170)

The fact that the status quo marginalizes the activities that lead to the condition of IT!—as jazz was marginalized as an expression of the African American experience (Baraka 1963)—is further evidence of the unnaturalness or unreasonableness of the status quo. Thus, the pursuit of IT! is, in many ways, the pursuit of sexual, spiritual, and political liberation.

Essayist Gregory Stephenson defines IT! in Eastern spiritual terms, explaining how IT! is "[t]he transcendence of personal, rational consciousness and the attainment of a synchronization with the infinite" (1990, 157). This conceptualization of Kerouac in terms of Eastern spirituality is important to emphasize since Kerouac, along with Gary Snyder and Alan Watts, is largely responsible for introducing Eastern mysticism and Zen Buddhism into the United States in the late 1950s (Jackson 1988; see also Rao 1974; Watts 1958). Kerouac's *Dharma Bums* (1958b), featuring Gary Snyder as the protagonist, is one of the first books in America, if not *the* first, to accentuate Eastern religious themes and infuse them in the popular mind. *Mexico City Blues* (1959b), a book of Kerouac's poetry, was an influential volume among poets of Kerouac's era, taking Eastern spirituality and giving it presence in American poetics, as well as in the American ecological movement.

The desire to reach a state of IT! is such a powerful force in *On the Road* that Sal and Dean are not content to reach IT! through the lone medium of music, or even meditation. As suggested, both characters attempt to recreate the experience of jazz rhapsody or meditative bliss in other, inventive ways. For example, Sal and Dean's experiences with marijuana, morphine, heroin, hallucinogenics, and excessive alcohol, their mad cross-country conversations, the mindless travel itself, and the energy portrayed in the book all attempt to approximate the Beat spiritual essence that transcends the mundane to become the IT! of unrestrained ecstasy.

While the specter of Dean's lost father is often eclipsed by the action of the text, and while it largely serves as a pretext for the travels and wanderings of the two men, it nevertheless motivates much of the action throughout the book.[9] A scene from the novel illustrates:

> [Dean speaking] "[B]ut hey, look down there in the night, thar, hup, hup, a buncha old bums by a fire by the rail, damn me." He almost slowed down. "You see, I never know whether my father's there or not." There were some figures by the tracks, reeling in front of a wood fire. "I never know whether to ask. He might be anywhere." We drove on. Somewhere behind us or in front of us in the huge night his father lay drunk under a bush, and no doubt about it—spittle on his chin, water on his pants, molasses in his ears, scabs on his nose, maybe blood in his hair and the moon shining down on him. (1957, 191)

Dean's lost father could be anywhere in America. Any bum or hobo that Sal and Dean meet could be Dean's father; hence all men need to be shown compassion. As he meets and mingles with these lost and hopeless figures, Sal muses that a bum can be anyone's father. Furthermore, since one of them produced Dean Moriarty, there must be something potentially great in each man. At moments such as these, Kerouac's Buddhist compassion becomes materialized. Indeed, it is a theme behind much of his writing.[10]

While Dean's derelict father represents a blessed figure, having created Dean and thus showing the potential for greatness in all men, and while the poor and the *fellahin* of the Earth (adapted from Spengler's *Decline of the West*) evoke Sal and Dean's compassion and respect, there is, nevertheless, the recalcitrant reality that the dispossessed must face on a daily level—a reality as harsh as it is romantic. This reality is never far from the characters of *On the Road*. This is most clear where Dean's father is concerned. Dean's father represents a reality that is close to Dean—a man chronically on the edge, a reminder that the liminal existence of social rootlessness leads finally to a condition of complete abandonment (discussed further in chapter 8).[11] Yet even in the ultimate state of deprivation and despair that the derelicts of society occupy, Kerouac discovers that there is a sense of freedom that an otherwise burdened man is denied. Dean suggests this liberating dimension of poverty though his unique life philosophy:

> "You see, man, you get older and troubles pile up. Someday you and me'll be coming down an alley together at sundown and looking in the cans to see." "You mean we'll end up old bums?" [asks Sal.] "Why not, man? Of course we will if we want to. . . . There's no harm ending that way. You spend a whole life of non-interference with the wishes of others, including politicians and the rich, and nobody bothers you and you cut along and make it your own way." (1957, 205)

In contrast with the warm, sentimental concern for Dean's lost father and the gentle romanticism of bums and the dispossessed in general, both Sal and Dean spend a great deal of energy in an attempt to achieve the state of IT! As mentioned above, IT! appears at the moments when action or experience come to a head, either through frantic activity, artistic rapture, or severe emotional strain. IT! represents the unpronounceable ecstasy that occurs when relentless souls merge their energies in jazz, sex, travel, drugs, or despair. In one poignant scene in *On the Road*, Sal describes the experience of IT! that he attains as he walks down the street in San Francisco, having been betrayed by Dean and left without money, friends, or a place to stay. Sal passes beyond a point of despair:

> [F]or a moment I had reached the point of ecstasy that I always wanted to reach, which was the complete step across chronological time into the timeless shadows, and wonderment in the bleakness of the mortal realm, and the sensation of death kicking at my heels to move on, with a phantom dogging its own heels, and myself hurrying to a plank where all the angels dove off and flew into the holy void of uncreated emptiness, the potent and inconceivable radiances shinning in the bright Mind Essence, innumerable lotus-lands falling open in the magic mothswarm of heaven. . . . I felt sweet, swinging bliss, like a big shot of heroin in the mainline vein; like a gulp of wine late in the afternoon and it makes you shudder; my feet tingled. I thought I was going to die the very next moment. (1957, 143)

As this passage illustrates, Kerouac and the Beats feel that life transcends into death and transformation; movement and change become the source of life, growth, and experience. This state of constant emotional upheaval, and its physical and psychological manifestations, contrasts with the static, controlled, and fabricated existence of 1950s corporate American culture.

As can be expected by the prose above, *On the Road* is a novel that ends without much resolution, in a traditional sense. Dean's father is never found. The pursuit of IT! culminates at frenzied intervals, but it is not permanent and soon passes. The mundane existence of everyday life always returns, leaving Sal and Dean no more the better and all the more worn down. Both characters experience sickness and disease in the novel. When Sal becomes too ill to travel, Dean abandons him again, this time in Mexico. In both cases, Sal is forgiving, recognizing that the holy madness of Dean must run its own course, unconstrained by even the bonds of friendship. Later, at the end of the book when Sal's disillusionment with Dean becomes more tangible, he chooses to leave Dean behind in the snow and goes off with a girl and another friend to a concert. Dean had suddenly come unannounced to New York one winter after he and Sal had made vague plans to live together in California. The men had been living on opposite coasts, working to earn money for the move. But Dean, always the compulsive, driven lunatic, irresponsibly arrives weeks early and all plans fall apart (as they always do in the novel). The novel ends with this disillusionment; the obscenity of Dean's lifestyle creates pressures that Sal can no longer accept. No certainty is presented at the novel's conclusion, no dramatic or climactic resolution of plot or character development. Without Dean to inspire him, Sal's energy and experience end, and the novel ends. Ostensibly, little is revealed to Sal or to Kerouac's reading audience besides the "forlorn rags of growing old" (1957, 254) that Sal accepts as he sits on a broken-down pier and ponders the random senselessness of our "Pooh-Bear" like existence.

The fact that *On the Road* presents no traditional resolution is not disturbing in the least, although it does contribute to the controversial style of the text. To those attuned to Kerouac's message and vision, the novel's end is a beginning, an invitation to change and transformation. Kerouac wrote the book as one chapter in a legend that he was designing and giving to the world. He saw his life as a legend and tried to give that legend a voice and a presence; his "road" books are all documentations of that legend. From *On the Road* the legend continued to unfold. More important, the novel represents the beginning of a new lifestyle, a consciousness that left the pages of Sal and Dean's adventures to become a force of its own life and own reckoning. "[N]othing ever ended" (1957,

248), Kerouac wrote, and for his vision that was certainly true. *On the Road* was the beginning of that vision's popular expression.[12]

Kerouac and the Beat Generation

Kerouac's life and work cannot be fully understood outside of the context of the Beat Generation, and his vision and rhetorical significance in contributing to an American counterculture must be situated in the Beat Generation so that its amplification and chaining-out effects can be placed in perspective.

Kerouac is widely recognized as the unlikely and resistant "leader" or "father" of the Beats, hailed in the popular media as the "King of the Beats."[13] However, this honorific title does not reflect his actual participation in what became popularized as the "Beat Generation"; by the time the Beats became a media phenomenon, Kerouac had retired and begun his rapid (and unromantic) descent into depression, decay, and death. Furthermore, Kerouac's label also results from an important misidentification: Kerouac was thought by many to exemplify the lifestyle that was led by Neal Cassady. The Beat Generation itself was an ideological community that defied a strict genealogical characterization. In reality, it was a loose connection of artists and alienated youth. Its unifying characteristic was its role in helping to shape American Left culture during the 1950s and 1960s. The Beat Generation gave the political Left a degree of cultural style during this time. Still, even with these qualifications, Kerouac *did*, at least for a time when he was unknown and actually living on the road, enact his vision. Karlyn Kohrs Campbell and Kathleen Jamieson discuss "enactment" as the process whereby rhetors "incarnate" their argument and embody "the proof of what is said" (1977, 9).

Through his art and life, Kerouac called into being a "community," however loosely we must use the term, and gave it an epistemological consciousness. Charters acknowledges Kerouac's unique position in the Beat Generation:

> In the intensity of the vision he had of his confused life he caught the dreams of a generation: the feeling that at some point something had been together, that there was a special vision they all shared, a romantic ideal that called on the road just ahead. To this generation Jack Kerouac became a romantic hero, an archetypal rebel, the symbol of their own vanities, the symbol of their own romantic legend. (1973, 22)

Reviewing Kerouac's book for the *New York Times*, Gilbert Millstein credits *On the Road* as being "the most beautifully executed, the clearest and the most important utterance yet made by the generation Kerouac himself named years ago as 'beat,' and whose principal avatar he is" (1957, 27). In "naming" this generation, Kerouac exerted influence on two generations of young people. This influence ranged from the beatniks to the hippies and from Greenwich Village to North Beach. As exemplified by Wavey Gravey, the hippie clown (and former Beat poet) who led the medical services at the original Woodstock music festival, Kerouac's influence reached far into the self-proclaimed "Woodstock Nation" (Cook 1971, 232). Indeed, during the 1960s, scores of social revolutions rose to rattle the cages of American conformity. While Kerouac's vision is alien to some of these movements (most notably the feminist movement, for obvious reasons), it is intimately tied to many (Oakley 1986).[14] Robert J. Milewsky substantiates the claim that Kerouac had a significant effect on American culture:

> Jack Kerouac, through his writing, exerted a force (or influence) on the outside world. The life-style of the Beats was emulated by the beatniks. They had their pads, poetry readings, beards, dark clothing, hot and cool jazz, chicks, slangs, parties, wine, marijuana, etc.; and all of this borrowed, largely, in itself from the bohemians, hipsters, and jazz musicians Kerouac knew and wrote about. (Later, the hippies of the sixties would adopt or transform some of these for their own use.) Also, the young of each generation since Kerouac have gone "on the road," across the country, exploring his America. *On the Road*, that Baedeker of beatism, became the traveler's guide of the penniless set, America's second and third generation "dharma bums." Kerouac became the "hero of the alienated." (1981, 7)

The social movements that Kerouac has been identified with, calling for reform, freedom, sexual liberation, and a new and less materialistic cultural outlook, were powerful enough to make a permanent mark on American culture and to usher in a range of resistance narratives and alternative lifestyles that were simply unthinkable in the drab grayness of 1950s America. Anthropologist Pierre Anctil describes how "Kerouac's experience . . . brutally highlights the post-war spectacle of a triumphant, arrogant and self-satisfied America comfortably installed in the contemplation of its material wealth" (1990, xviii). In contrast to this brutality and base arrogance, Kerouac served as a central point of resistance, emphasizing compassion and diversity. As Anctil concludes, "By virtue of a great adventurer . . . Kerouac denounced this new asphyxia and gave force to the call of the wild, in all its purity" (xix). In exhorting America to actualize a new purity of heart and cultural expression, Kerouac contributed to a symbolic restructuring of American values. Allen Ginsberg explains this idea more fully and further documents the direct genealogical connections between the Beats and the hippies:

> I don't think it is possible to proceed further in America without first understanding Kerouac's tender brooding compassion for bygone scene & personal Individuality oddity'd therein. Bypassing Kerouac one bypasses the mortal heart, sung in prose vowels . . . a giant mantra of appreciation and adoration of an American man, one striving heroic soul. Kerouac's judgment on Neal Cassady was confirmed by later [Ken] Kesey history. (1972, vii)

Kerouac's relationship to the Beat Generation, and the relationship between the Beat Generation and the larger, more socially diverse counterculture of the 1960s, can be seen rhetorically, as this study documents. In particular, Ernest G. Bormann's theory of fantasy theme and rhetorical vision helps explain the process behind this rhetorical influence. As he explains, "When a person appropriates a rhetorical vision he gains with the supporting dramas constraining forces which impel him to adopt a lifestyle and to take certain action" (1972, 406). In the case of Kerouac, this vision enabled people to become aware of their option to adopt different lifestyles and gave them the opportunity to join with the "drama" that was formed by a new way of viewing reality. Bormann explains, "[T]he convert to one of the counter cultures in the 1960s would let his hair and beard grow, change his style of dress, and his method of work" (407). Readers of Kerouac would become transformed into "Beats" and later into "hippies" as changes in their attitudes became manifested in behavioral and lifestyle changes.[15] These changes would, circularly, effect and reinforce attitudinal commitments. Ironically, however, while these "converts" were seeking freedom from societal norms and the establishment of their own individuality and values, the shifting of narratives brought with it, as it always does, a shifting of constraints. As Michel Foucault warns, there is no "liberation" in the sense that a new value system and set of social beliefs can bring "freedom." Rather, all epistemologies have their blinders and their boundaries (see Foucault 1980; Burke 1984). More specifically, as Maurice Charland warns, "Subjects within narratives are not free, they are positioned and so constrained. All narratives have power over the subjects they present" (1987, 140). Thus, Kerouac's narrative, the visions and fantasies promoted in his text, while suggesting new avenues of cultural and personal expression, also serve to limit action and to reify belief. The limitations of the politically Left counterculture and its relative wane in influence since the 1970s may be due in part to the fact that narratives provide their own limited and limiting social apparatuses. In other words, countercultures themselves need to be re-envisioned from time to time to avoid suffocating in their own stagnated reifications.

3

Kerouac's Rhetorical Situation

"**R**hetoric" is defined as a system of influence, conscious or unconscious, that persuaders, including cultural persuaders such as artists, writers, and teachers, exert through the narrowing and accentuating of social/symbolic reality. In this sense, *On the Road* is a rhetorical text because, through it, Kerouac constructs systems of meaning that influence a reader's life decisions, structures of influence to direct action, and an ideology to promote and maintain a coherent and encompassing worldview or epistemology. Above all else, rhetoric involves a rationality, but one without its traditional foundations in a transcendent, Cartesian Reason. Rhetoric encourages a localized rationality, built from specific wants and needs, that advances a communal consciousness. Rhetoric constructs social visions of the "good" and the "just."

In chapter 2, I situated Kerouac in the cultural milieu of his time. Rhetorical artifacts and appeals are, by definition, historical. The qualities of any type of rhetorical transaction can be recognized only as they take place in time. When the temporal element is lost, rhetorical elements blend indistinguishably from the flora of other symbols. This is specifically Foucault's point in *The Order of Things* (1970) when he highlights the role of history in giving substance to our understanding of texts. Texts, such as the incomprehensible ancient Chinese encyclopedia Foucault holds up as an example, exist as physical objects. Yet the meaning of this encyclopedia, as well as its rhetorical or informative structure, is lost when its context is lost (xv–xix). The loss of context is like the loss of a language; the link between commonality and rationality is broken between two worlds. Knowledge, after all, proceeds by semblance and metaphor (Rosmarin 1985). A person's rationality, a person's rhetoric, is his or her ability to see relationships among uncommon things. History is the barrier and the bridge between such understandings.[1]

As a methodology, fantasy theme criticism is a useful heuristic for understanding a rhetorical artifact. In particular, fantasy theme analysis is a way to understand the historical context that gives structure and meaning to Kerouac's vision. The method, as any critical method, does not lead to the "Truth." Rather, *all* methods of inquiry do one thing and only one thing well: they provide interested people with specific localized frameworks to help structure their interpretative understandings of "the world." All research methodologies work to better or worse degree for different tasks, but their primary goal is to introduce the scholar to natural or social phenomena. Not all methods are equally useful; but then again, neither is all scholarship. A method's usefulness, as is a scholar's usefulness, is measured by the work that is generated. All research, all knowledge, serves some function; otherwise it would be unrecognizable.[2]

Kerouac, Culture, and the 1960s

American culture in the 1960s was turbulent (Viorst 1979). The brutality and hypocrisy of American domestic and foreign policy became a focal point for discussion and resistance. Dissent was open and at times violent; the times were violent; the government was violent. America festered and bled. "Peace" and "justice" were fought for, both on the national and international fronts—in Vietnam by the Vietnamese who rose to resist French and then American imperialism, and in the streets of the United States by Americans of African descent who were trying to throw off the yoke of a bitter racism (King 1992). It seemed to many people that the system was no longer working, that it did not work morally. Some progressive people came to feel that the systemic despair and hopelessness of the old order could be redescribed with great visions of peace, freedom, and diversity. A revolutionary atmosphere was prevalent. This was a period of time in U.S. history when the promise of an encompassing and popular democracy had its potential. This was not a dream democracy that was being forged in the streets during this time but a *real* one that was alive with potential and hope. Ultimately, it was a democracy that failed.

The social unrest that swept through America surprised those who did not have the foresight to see that a society based on lies, deceit, imperialism, commercialism, racism, and sexism cannot easily live with its contradictions (see Chomsky 1988). The FBI and the CIA worked together, along with other right-wing groups and reactionary forces, to stifle, to smother, to force into submission many people who dreamed of a better future for themselves and for others (Blackstock 1988; Churchill and Wall

1988, 1990). Sadly, the lessons and moral growth of the 1960s are easily forgotten, especially since the Reagan presidency and the subsequent rollback of many social gains and popular political consciousness.

The 1960s were about the development of a political/class consciousness among long-ignored segments of society who formed liberation movements with a newfound sense of enthusiasm and urgency. As Dr. Martin Luther King Jr. warned from the foot of the Lincoln Memorial, "It would be fatal for the nation to overlook the urgency of the moment" (1992, 103). King was correct. The urgency of the 1960s was clear, the malignancy of neglect was real, and the nation—meaning our political and economic leaders—failed to rise to the occasion (see King 1968). Many ideas, norms, and expectations that had been held in high national esteem were seriously called into question but ultimately reaffirmed.

A discussion of Kerouac is germane to the above but with some important qualifications. First, all of this is *more* than Kerouac. Kerouac was writing his most important books in the early 1950s, and his experiences that informed his books took place in the late 1940s. Kerouac was writing from a different world with different experiences than the world of the late 1960s. Furthermore, Kerouac was not writing about "justice" and "equality," or even about "class consciousness." Kerouac was not a social theorist or a revolutionary, as were Che Guevara or Stokely Carmichael; he was not a leader in the sense of Martin Luther King Jr.; he never had the wide appeal that John Lennon cultivated. So how do I justify tying *On the Road* into the larger cultural and political realms?

My answer to the question of how a more democratic, progressive, and economically just politics relates to Kerouac involves the fact that democratic politics, economic fairness, equal rights, and U.S. imperialism are all related. Freedom in the United States, social diversity, and tolerance all involve the same political equation, centering on human values and ideology (both in the sense of a productive consciousness and of a "false" consciousness). In short, Kerouac played an important role in focusing popular awareness on the question of values. The political and social revolts of the 1960s were first and foremost revolts in value, revolts leading to an awareness of oppression and death and of alternatives. This popular questioning of values began in the late 1950s, long before the Vietnam War erupted into the living rooms and consciousness of the American people.

The initial questioning of dominant American values in the 1950s involved responses to the decay of culture under industrialism and commercialism, as well as to the rise of suburban life (both of which were made possible, if we take Noam Chomsky seriously, by the Third World empire that the United States seized as its spoils of World War II).[3] The dominant culture of commercialism and suburbia was reified and grounded in myths and rationalizations that served two purposes: they limited thought by making it seem as if the world as *presented* was the world as it *has to be*, and they helped to obscure the terrible price paid for corporate and commercial America among the disenfranchised. These myths or rationalizations serve as fantasy themes for the particular narratives that justified the status quo. For example, in post-World War II America, Dwight D. Eisenhower exemplified the superficial cool, orderly nature of contemporary culture at the time. Americans were told to "like" Ike, and all would be okay with the world. Ike looked after us, made us safe and secure. Never mind that "safety" and "security" were premised on the notion that what was good for America was what was good for American corporations.

This ideology of selfishness and materialism is further exemplified in literature (see Wilson 1955; Whyte 1956). For example, Sloan Wilson's *The Man in the Gray Flannel Suit* explores and typifies the psyche of the middle-class experience: the protagonist, Thomas R. Rath, a war hero struggling with the demands of post-war life in America, declares, "We might as well admit that what we want is a big house and a new car and trips to Florida in the winter, and plenty of life insurance" (1955, 10). These are false needs; they are corporate, designed, and intentional. They are the result of ad campaigns, propaganda, and a value system that accepts and encourages the rape of the Earth and the colonization of others (Stauber and Rampton 1995). The growth of industry that was stimulated by the success of World War II and by Cold War imperialism promoted the surface appearance of control over the environment that technology represented. This was an age before the publication of Rachel Carson's *Silent Spring* (1962), when the promise of science and technology reigned golden like an Olympic god. Anticipating a new consciousness that encouraged a skepticism of science and an increased respect for the Earth, Kerouac and the Beats questioned the mythology of the American Holy Trinity—Progress, Money, Science. In this context, *On the Road* becomes an important political document. It brought to the forefront of our national consciousness an alternative way of wanting, of knowing. Barry Gifford and Lawrence Lee distinguish between the two consciousnesses that Kerouac's book polarizes:

> The America Kerouac portrayed in *On the Road* was an entirely different country from Eisenhower's America, which received the book. The novel was a traveler's tale from an alternate nation with the same language, cities, highways, and movie stars that its readers were familiar with, but separated in some important way from the motives and energies that drove most Americans of the 1950s. (1978, 231)

In separating his characters from the dominant culture of America, Kerouac helps introduce into popular literature the questioning of the old myths. It is this act of questioning that is revolutionary. Fires start with sparks, which are very small. More specifically, by questioning the myths or values of a society or culture, rhetors focus attention to new ground on which the construction of social reality can take place. For instance, Michael McGee observes how the questioning of a "myth" can introduce "crisis" and lead ultimately to the development of a new vision:

> Each political myth presupposes a "people" who can legislate reality with their collective belief. So long as "the people" believe basic myths, there is unity and collective identity. When there is no fundamental belief, one senses a crisis which can only be met with a new rhetoric, a new mythology. (1975, 245)

Kerouac's fundamental role in helping to encourage the events of the 1960s was his suggestion that there was no unity, no collective identity to which every American had to proclaim his or her loyalty. He challenged the fundamental beliefs of his time, thus suggesting that a new reality could be constructed. Certainly, much of what happened in the 1960s had nothing to do with Kerouac and would have happened had he never been born; nevertheless, such circumstances would have been *different*. Kerouac tilled the soil and sowed the seeds for much of the visionary discourse that took place after him. Gary Snyder substantiates the claim that Kerouac's Beat Generation exceeded its 1950s role and grew, myth-like, to something larger and more consequential. When asked in an interview what happened to the Beat Generation, Snyder replied, "[I]t transformed into the hippie-generation and continued . . . and it reaches out and connects with the peace movement, the civil rights movement, [and] ultimately with the ecology movement" (qtd. in Lauridsen and Dalgard 1990, 69). Dennis Sean McNally concurs with Snyder when he writes, "In a strange marriage, the Beats and Kennedy liberalism had together given birth to the 'Movement,' a loose connection of antiwar, anti-poverty, and civil rights groups" (1979, 312).

This "Movement" and its progenitors, the Beats, were not universally embraced by members of the literary and cultural establishment. Kerouac, in particular, suffered from the criticism directed at popular dissent. Largely due to *On the Road* and the media attention that it attracted, Kerouac became a national anathema to the conservative forces of this country who felt threatened by his questioning of societal norms. In part because of the messages in *On the Road*, and possibly because the establishment was looking for a scapegoat to blame for the rise of such social ills as juvenile delinquency and violence (which have structural, systemic causes that are frequently mystified), influential figures of the literary and cultural establishment rose to criticize Kerouac, as they continue to do today.

Podhoretz and Will: The Conservative Response

The conservative response to Kerouac stretches much farther than did his active presence in American culture. The two clearest examples of such conservative responses are from Norman Podhoretz (1958) and George Will (1988). Thirty years separate these critics' observations, and yet they are remarkably consistent. Podhoretz and Will also represent, generally speaking, opposite places on the political spectrum, a clear indication of how American politics has collapsed the significant distinctions between "liberal" and "conservative" positions.

Criticism of Kerouac, and of the social movement/consciousness he exemplified in 1957, began almost immediately upon the publication of *On the Road*. Its clearest early expression can be found in "The Know-Nothing Bohemians," a 1958 essay by literary critic Podhoretz. Generally associated with "liberal" politics, Podhoretz frequently contributed to *Commentary*, where he also served as editor. In his article, he judges the Beat Generation, and Kerouac in particular, as indicative of the rise of gang violence seen in the 1950s. Podhoretz equates the "Primitivism" he sees in Kerouac's writing with the breakdown of law and order:

> The reason why I bring this up is that the spirit of hipsterism and the Beat Generation strikes me as the same spirit which animates the young savages in leather jackets who have been running amok in the last few years with their switchblades and zip guns. (1958, 318)

Kerouac is singled out by Podhoretz as exemplifying an implicit, antiintellectual, murderous rage:

> Even the relatively mild ethos of Kerouac's books can spill over easily into brutality, for there is a suppressed cry in those books: Kill the intellectuals who can talk coherently, kill the people who can sit still for five minutes at a time, kill those incomprehensible characters who are capable of getting seriously involved with a woman, a job, a cause. (1958, 318)

Never mind that *On the Road* contains a minimum amount of violence, which takes place in one bar scene (46–47), and that, far from acting belligerently, the characters of the novel shirk confrontation, as they shirk responsibility in general. Indeed, the characters, while "morally" loose in terms of their attitudes toward sex and drugs, seem resolved to renounce violence. Kerouac, a student of Catholicism and Buddhism, was benevolent, and his writing appeals to compassion and understanding.[4]

In light of Kerouac's avowed passivity and the anti-war position of the Beats and hippies, the extremity of Podhoretz's character assassination of Kerouac demands further investigation. Kerouac is no knife-wielding hoodlum, any more so than is Podhoretz. In terms of the different ideologies that Kerouac and Podhoretz support, Podhoretz is probably more guilty than is Kerouac of cultivating or contributing to an atmosphere of terror. For example, throughout the 1970s and 1980s, Podhoretz exemplified the blind and dogmatic support for the Israeli policy of oppressing the Palestinians and for other warlike stances taken toward the Arab world (Podhoretz 1982; Chomsky 1983).[5]

Critics can use cultural analysis to reveal the border between politics and art (as discussed in more detail below). All critical stances are political, even overtly political. Podhoretz's contempt for Kerouac in the late 1950s and, by extension, his contempt for radical democratic or other leftist politics (under the guise of a "liberal" position) is related to his work as a cultural critic and his later anti-human rights, anti-Palestinian politics. Podhoretz is a clear example of how "progressive" politics in the United States has been marginalized from "acceptable" politics. What remains is two shades of conservatism. What is lost is imaginative, innovative, and transformational politics.

Podhoretz himself accentuates the connection between art and politics, or at least art and behavior, when he attributes to Kerouac an explicit attack on law and order. Indeed, my retort to Podhoretz is not that he is wrong for making this connection. The link between art and politics does exist; his particular claims about Kerouac, however, are absurd and sensationalist. Podhoretz's response, while representing an extreme example of the animosity directed toward Kerouac, highlights the concern felt by the more conservative sections of society about the effects of people like Kerouac on culture. Kerouac *is* dangerous, just like Podhoretz is dangerous (as far as the Palestinians are concerned). Both men are "dangerous" to the extent that they help to inform our decisions, help to create the avenues upon which we understand our available options.[6]

Specifically, Kerouac is dangerous because his idea of life and culture does not support the traditional notions of law and order that reify an economic world that depends on marriage, work, military aggression, and conformity. That is what makes Kerouac a threat: he invites, entertains, and seriously evokes an alternative life that deprives the cultural and political elites of their ability to enforce their will. In contrast, Kerouac ushers in a new era of change, of epistemological flexibility and of compassion. For many, Kerouac represents a break with the bourgeois life, no less than he represents a break with Marxism as an epistemology. Indeed, traditional Marxists have no use for Kerouac. They see him as irresponsible, immature, and, ultimately, just as dangerous as they would see Podhoretz and Will. Kerouac is dangerous to *any* system, on the Right or the Left, that is not flexible with its value assumptions. But Kerouac is not critiquing a Communist epistemology in *On the Road*. His critique is of capitalism and of a capitalist society that he sees as spiritually unreasonable.

That Kerouac's ideology is not Marxist makes him no less a threat to capitalism. He does the one thing that cannot be tolerated by any repressive society: he suggests alternatives to traditional values and questions the ruling society's right to authority. Consequently, while Kerouac's books are innovative and continue to be read and studied, there is considerable hesitancy, even today, to give recognition to Kerouac the man. Years after the last remnants of popular social revolt have subsided in the dominant media, Kerouac's influence is resented in some segments of society among people who view the 1960s as an era best left unremembered. George F. Will's unprovoked polemic against Kerouac in *Newsweek* typifies this sentiment:

> There is nothing so easily effected or so undemanding as membership in a generation. And the self-dramatization of a generation has never been more relentless than that of "the '60s generation." The self-congratulation of that generation goes on ad nauseam. In fact, the worst feature of the '50s is that they were pregnant with the '60s. (1988, 64)

As Podhoretz before him, Will sees Kerouac as representing something alien and, thirty years after Kerouac published *On the Road*, is compelled to continue Podhoretz's critique against Kerouac. Will's polemic represents another point that Chomsky continually makes: it is not enough for the state to "win" and dismantle a vision; the propaganda of the state requires that people even stop *thinking* about the potential or promise that lies in a defeated progressive movement. Popular movements are defeated and demonized, and people are led to believe that no viable alternative exists to the status quo.

As is the case with Podhoretz, the severity and unreasonableness of Will's attack on Kerouac, particularly in light of the 1988 cultural landscape, suggests that we need to look deeper into Will's remarks. Kenneth

Burke teaches us that when the intensity of a writer's language is out of proportion to the obvious context, something deeper is at work. For instance, notice how Will staunchly opposes the thesis of this book: membership in a generation is "undemanding," he argues. I have been arguing that membership in a generation is a creative act that demands significant rhetorical and ideological commitment. Yet "rhetoric" and "ideology" are things that conservatives like Will do not recognize as existing; they are little more than "self-dramatization" or silly, inconsequential things that interfere with mature people leading responsible lives. Dramatization is equated with "self-congratulation," a self-serving and ungrounded flattery.

For Will, the 1950s and 1960s were marked by an absence of positive influences—as if civil rights, opposition to the Vietnam War and to the military/industrial complex, free speech, black power, women's liberation, gay liberation, and a growing ecological sensitivity are insignificant developments in the United States. In a sense, they *are* insignificant, depending upon how one defines what the United States *is*. If the U.S. is a progressive nation among the nations of the world, a country devoted to liberty, freedom, and moral excellence, then, indeed, the popular and grass-roots social agitation of the 1960s must be counted as a significant advancement of those goals. If, however, the United States is a capitalist power devoted to the worldwide maintenance of class structure, and if its government is run by and for the interest of the business elites who control the world's resources, then the development of democratic and social consciousness that marked the 1960s must be seen as abhorrent by those in power, those who are privileged to decide what is counted as "history." In this context, the consciousness of the 1960s must be contained, reversed, erased from memory.

Will's observations of the 1950s and 1960s, while unprovoked in the already secure and repressive political environment of the Reagan presidency, are not without context. Will is responding to the efforts of people in Lowell, Massachusetts, to honor Jack Kerouac, that community's most well known son. In 1988, the people of Lowell, in pride, dedicated a small park, Eastern Canal Park, to Kerouac. This dedication created backlash, and Will rose to the occasion. In his *Newsweek* column, Will castigates the event, declaring, "Lowell's little park is one more sign that America is making a cottage industry out of recycled radicalisms" (1988, 64).

Notice the language of marginalization as well as the tone of Will's observation. For Will, it is not enough that the gains of the 1960s have been rolled back; rather, we must ritualistically sneer at even the memory of those who dared envision and articulate what they believed was a better life. In this way, the status quo can co-opt whatever positive residues remain after the heroic striving of people to improve their lives is down-played in an effort to obliterate their memory. This point is particularly important and can use some further examples.

A clear instance of how the systemic co-optation of edifying ideas and cultural positions encourages a lapse in historical memory is "Loyalty Day," a holiday celebrated on May 1, proclaimed by Congress on July 18, 1958, to eviscerate the political significance of May Day, the inter-national working-class holiday. As the Honorable James E. Van Zandt remarked in Congress during discussion of the holiday, "Loyalty Day, May 1, as a counter observance to the May Day celebration of the Com-munists, provides an appropriate occasion to lay stress on our blessings as a people" (1958, 8182). The effort to downplay or co-opt the inter-national workers' holiday remains today. In 1994, Clinton honored Loy-alty Day with these words: "Each year, at the height of spring's renewal, Americans take the time to reaffirm our allegiance to our country and to the ideals upon which it was founded." Spring renewal seems so nice and innocent, and the reification of an acceptable holiday is complete; there is no mention in this public document of the working-class conscious-ness that the president is successfully mystifying. Van Zandt, in the con-gressional debates, was more honest in his desire to co-opt the energy and attention generated by May Day and to channel it into affirmations of patriotism and loyalty.

An even clearer example of how forces of the status quo co-opt posi-tive residues of controversial cultural artifacts can be found in advertis-ing. Consider, for instance, a six-page Volvo ad that appears in the De-cember 25, 1995, issue of *Time* magazine (as well as in other popular publications). On the first page of the ad are three pictures and the words, "A moment in the life of a car company." The first picture is a young couple getting married, the second is the man ("John") and woman ("Connie") embracing, and the third is a twenty-seven-year-old copy of *On the Road*. Two pages of the ad comprise a narrative centering on Kerouac and his place in this couple's life. The narrative hearkens back to an earlier time when, driving his father's Volvo, the young man in the ad (now old as revealed in a subsequent photograph) and his girlfriend (now lifelong mate) decide spontaneously to get married in Las Vegas. Against this backdrop is the sentence, "The only sounds that could be heard were the words of Kerouac and the heartbeat of two people about to begin life together."

The present in this narrative is 1995, three decades after the previous elopement. The couple is now retired; their kids have grown and moved out on their own. However, some things have not changed with the years; for example, the couple is still excited about owning a Volvo. In their Volvo, they make the same trip they took years earlier when they got

36

married, perhaps to reaffirm their marriage vows on their thirtieth anniversary. The narrator, a public relations person from Volvo, explains: "Always the romantic, John remembered to bring *On the Road*. Not one of those new printings he'd seen in the bookstore at the mall but the original one that he had stored away in the attic."[7] John then reads from the book, the passage on page 9 where Kerouac describes scrambling after the mad people who live and burn and explode like Roman candles in the night (not exactly ideal marriage material). "As she finishes mouthing the words with him, Connie quietly whispers, 'That's beautiful.'"

Besides the obvious incongruities of this narrative, such as Kerouac being evoked to lend inspiration for a spontaneous marriage, Volvo poaches the mystique of Kerouac, creating an exhilarating ethos for its product. In the process, Volvo rapes Kerouac's vision of a society that rejects commodification. Kerouac never advanced a romanticism of the car, and he never owned an automobile. Even Neal Cassady cared little for an automobile; he drove his cars so hard that they often fell apart in his hands. The object of Kerouac's mystique was not the automobile; it was the freedom that comes from not being attracted to material goods. Kerouac traveled by foot, by bus, and by hitchhiking. If anything, Kerouac romanticized the hoboes, the people who *walked* across America or rode in boxcars, free from responsibility and worry. In *On the Road*, Dean Moriarty *stole* cars; the one car he actually purchased was repossessed because he could not make the payments.

Both Loyalty Day and the Volvo ad marginalize dissent and propagate a countervision that supports the status quo. This is a pattern in American political culture: reform is often demonized and the counterpersuasion manages to place the original reformers in a defensive position or into a negative or irrelevant cultural light. In the first example, working-class consciousness/solidarity is reduced to Communism. In the second, *On the Road* is refashioned as an anachronistic dream text, the inspiration for a spontaneous yet highly successful marriage. In each case, the original point is lost. May Day is about improving the condition of workers across the world, and *On the Road* is about rejecting the commitments of marriage and commercialism.

In a similar fashion, Will's editorial is strategically placed. For Will, Kerouac's park represents, and is reduced to, a "cottage industry," and the memory evoked by a community proud of one of its children is chastised for recycling radicalism. The park cannot just be a park, and Kerouac's memory cannot be taken as just something special to the people of Lowell, Massachusetts. Rather, the park becomes a symbol for something else, something that makes Lowell's pride and meager park seem diabolical.

The park becomes a symbol of radicalism and must be marginalized, pushed from any type of public forum or cultural consideration. Radicalism, in the sense that it is negatively evoked by Will, is something cheap to begin with; recycling it only magnifies its absurdity. Rather, radicalism is something to be discarded, an unusable relic from an unremarkable time. Indeed, the concept of recycling is, itself, an absurd concept in a culture based on gross, mass consumerism. In his 1932 warning about the trends then obvious in Western culture, Aldous Huxley (1969) described a future world of consumption where "more stitches" equals "less riches." Huxley's sentiment helps reveal some of the indignation that we find in Will's polemic.[8]

In a telling paragraph, Will elaborates upon why Kerouac is not worthy of recognition in his hometown:

> [T]his native was not a political or military leader, a captain of industry, or, truth be told, a man of large and lasting accomplishments in the arts. He is remembered less because of what he produced than because he seems, in retrospect, to have been a portent of cultural storms. (1988, 64)

Notice what Will is attempting to express. For him, the 1960s was a cultural "storm," a turbulence to be weathered. The metaphor of a "storm" suggests dark violence and senseless destruction. Storms pass, leaving a mess to clean up; but, nevertheless, people are relieved and get back to the business of their lives. Storms are inconveniences, nothing more. For Will, the 1960s stand out as a passing turbulence, a darkness that breaks in the light of day and reason. As Michael Osborn argues, the use of such metaphors are not inconsequential; they suggest a *weltanschauung* and "permit a more precise focusing upon whatever values and motives are salient in society at a given time" (1967, 126).

In addition to collapsing all progressive political, social, and cultural activity in the 1960s into a single storm metaphor to marginalize and to alienate those activities, Will reveals further assumptions about *who* can be considered important in American culture. To be somebody worth remembering, a person must be a political, military, or industrial leader—in short, a person must be wealthy. Traditionally, that means a person must be a white male. In addition, that person must be a Republican or a Democrat, since a nonpolitically aligned person (or one whose politics are not approved) would find it difficult to gain a position of significant political or military responsibility. In addition, a socialist or anarchist would find it difficult to acquire industrial power. According to Will, the only area in which non-white, rich Democratic or Republican men or women can gain some sort of cultural respect is in the arts. But there are significant qualifications here as well, the most important being "permanence." Yet to have "lasting influence" means to have one's work recognized as meaningful by a culture's opinion leaders. Not surprising, community "taste" is often prescribed by the norms of the status quo, which, in the case of the United States, happens to be largely controlled by rich white men who are Democrats and Republicans. So where does Will make room for people like Kerouac? While Kerouac is white and male, he is by no means rich and Republican (although he did affiliate with Republican values in the last alcoholic years of his life).[9] Simply put, Will's idea of cultural significance reflects an epistemology rejected by Kerouac and his work and by the Beats. This leads to a discussion of art and ideology.

Art and Ideology

In many respects, the countercultural Left was a response to the mentality of people like Podhoretz and Will. This counterculture rejected traditional political, military, and industrial leadership and turned instead to other conceptualizations of authority (as elaborated upon in chapter 5). Will's notion of art is also exceedingly conservative and limiting of human experience—a limitation of consciousness that Beat poetry expressively rejected (Jones 1992).

Will's view maintains that art is ahistorical (or at least it has ahistorical qualities); in order to be considered "True," the norms and accomplishments of art must exhibit "lasting" significance. The cash value of art is its permanence: the more impermanent the art, the less its value, the more its significance is illusory. Will's position on art, like his political position, is Platonic; it is based on a system of hierarchies and "natural" orders. This position is clearly articulated by Richard M. Weaver, one of the intellectual fathers of the neoconservatism for which Will is an apologist. According to Weaver:

> Rational society is a mirror of the logos, and this means that it has a formal structure which enables apprehension. The preservation of society is therefore directly linked with the recovery of true knowledge. . . . If society is something which can be understood, it must have structure; if it has structure, it must have hierarchy; against this metaphysical truth the declamations of the Jacobins break in vain. (1948, 35)

Within such a hierarchy, value exists relative to an object's position. The higher up the hierarchy one ascends, the better understanding one has of the way things *are*. These things do not change; they are permanent and are not subject to social influences.

With a metaphysical commitment to hierarchy and permanence, Will does not recognize that art can be, first and foremost, social. As I argue in an essay on Burke's theory of form, art is exceedingly social (Swartz 1996a). Its effects and its appeals are always historically contextualized. As Burke explains:

> Aesthetic values are intermingled with ethical values—and the ethical is the basis of the practical. Or, put more simply: our ideas of the beautiful, the curious, the interesting, the unpleasant, the boring are closely bound with our ideas of the good, the desirable, the undesirable—and our ideas of the desirable and undesirable have much to do with our attitudes towards our everyday activities. They make us ask ourselves, more or less consciously: Are we doing the things we want to do? [T]o what extent is there a breach between what we must do and what we should like to do? Probably for this reason, even the most practical of revolutions will generally be found to have manifested itself first in the "aesthetic" sphere. (1973, 234)

While Western models of art continue to enthrall us, from Greek statues and architecture to Renaissance paintings and music, they do not do so because such forms, what we consider to be "masterpieces," are ahistorical. Rather, what we misinterpret as their "permanence" is an element of strong cultural resonance. By our standards, our art seems to be eternal; we simply would not be *we* if this did not appear to be the case. Art is permanent only to the extent that the people who create that art remain. As the people change, as each generation of people "become," aesthetic and artistic norms change. Where they remain consistent, as in the example of Greek and Renaissance art, strong historical consciousness exists, even though this consciousness becomes masked in the language of essentialism.

All art, however, has cultural resonance when it is created, at least to the extent that it is recognized and accepted as art, or even as "good" art. Similarly, Kerouac's particular importance is that his art had a strong cultural resonance at its time and continues to have a cultural relevance today, albeit a diminishing one. As Burke explains, literature, or art generally, functions to equip people for life's demands; it is "equipment for living" (1973, 293). Art, therefore, is rhetorical: it helps mediate conditions of acceptance and response. Specifically, Burke is discussing proverbs, but his message is no less applicable to extended narratives, such as a novel. Burke sees literature or art as "medicine" that is "designed for admonition or exhortation, for foretelling" (293). In addition, literature or art is only effective to the extent that it "sizes up" a social situation or structure, naming it, calling it into being. As Burke explains:

> Social structures give rise to "type" situations, subtle subdivisions of the relationships involved in competitive and cooperative acts.

> Many proverbs seek to chart, in more or less homey and picturesque
> ways, these "type" situations. I submit that such naming is done, not
> for the sheer glory of the thing, but because of its bearing upon hu-
> man welfare. (294)

Burke's discussion of literature as equipment for living takes us back
to our discussion in chapter 1 about naming. He explains how literature
is a form of rhetoric:

> [Art] is the strategic naming of a situation. It singles out a pattern
> of experience that is sufficiently representative of our social struc-
> ture, that recurs sufficiently often *mutandis mutatis*, for people to
> "need a word for it" and to adopt an attitude towards it. (300)

Literature, or art, is social because, as my analysis of *On the Road*
suggests, its success corresponds to a naming, an accentuation of something noteworthy in the world. Even romance novels, as a genre of literature, must be seen as social: they call into focus a certain sensitivity
(or sensibility), they direct action (or anticipation) by focusing on fantasy and bringing the romantic to the fore of a reader's consciousness
(Alberts 1986; Doyle 1985; Hubbard 1985).

In a similar fashion, Kerouac's *On the Road* foregrounds another type
of fantasy with more significant political implications than the typical
Harlequin romance novel, and he makes that fantasy "real" for his audience. Although each individual instance of art may have different de-
grees of social consequence and influence, art, in principle, is never in-
nocuous. Kerouac's books, as well as Harlequin romance novels, are
strategic attempts to reify a relationship that people can have with the
world. At the very least, they reinforce stereotypes about how the world
is and what is considered appropriate behavior. All books have this character, regardless of content. Obviously, unread books do not have any
influence, but the ideas contained within books, even those that do not
have a wide readership, often seep out and take on a life of their own.
Romance novels, like network soap operas (Rosen 1986), serve a real-
life function for certain people, or else they would not be produced.

Perhaps a romance novel, or any novel for that matter, can be read
and put down without significantly affecting its readers. Similarly, *On
the Road* could have bored some people, entertained others, and still have
had no effect on their lives; the mere existence of a text and its circulation
within a culture does not guarantee rhetorical significance. Novels, after
all, are not bullets or bombs, which have a much more direct influence
on the lives of people with whom they come into contact. The success or
worth of a rhetorical artifact can never be judged upon the totality of its

influence. By such criteria, we would have to reject not only every piece of art but almost every piece of cultural knowledge as well, because few, if any, truths, facts, or cultural phenomena exist with unanimous certainty or universal acclaim. There simply are no ahistorical foundations from which the art or knowledge of the world can be appreciated (cf. Rorty 1979). Rather, persuasive discourse must be analyzed for its potential to speak and to persuade and for the breadth and depth of its analysis.

In response to critics such as Podhoretz and Will and their contemptuous attacks on Kerouac and, by extension, the Left in general, chapters 5, 6, and 7 explore Kerouac's rhetorical vision and the social reality he helped to create. Kerouac's vision directly opposes the mind-set of a nation represented by the writings of Podhoretz and Will. Indeed, the negative press Kerouac received only brings home the point that, as Chris Challis recalls in his evaluation of Kerouac's career, "The Prophet is without honor in his own land" (1984, 175).

4

Fantasy, Rhetorical Vision, and the Critical Act

My main instrument for evaluating Kerouac's vision derives from Ernest G. Bormann's theorizing on fantasy theme analyses.[1] In his provocative 1972 essay, "Fantasy and Rhetorical Vision: The Rhetorical Criticism of Social Reality," Bormann extends from the pathbreaking work of psychologist Robert Bales in *Personality and Interpersonal Behavior*. In this chapter, I develop my methodological assumptions and review the general literature on fantasy theme analysis.

According to Bormann, Bales made a critical contribution to understanding group behaviors by discovering how "investigations of small group communication provide insight into the nature of public address and mass communication" (1972, 396). For Bales, as Bormann points out, the connection between small groups of people interacting and the influence of these groups on a larger audience can be understood in terms of "fantasy themes." Fantasy themes are the units of exchange, the negotiated currency that connects alienated people to each other. Fantasy themes help people to bridge their alienation and to build a communal and thus communicative consciousness. When amplified, this consciousness has the potential to spread. As Bormann explains, "Group fantasizing correlates with individual fantasizing and extrapolates to speaker-audience fantasizing and to the dream merchants of the mass media" (1972, 396).

The amplification of interpersonal processes that takes place in the mass media involves what is traditionally known as "rhetoric." Amplification involves transcendence and influence, structure and strategy. As

Richard Buchanan explains, "Amplification is the device for extending the scope of rhetoric from words to actions, thoughts, and things" (1996, 426). It invites response, integration, questioning, and resistance. Amplification, in short, calls out to be heard; it encourages participation. In this way, as well as in others, fantasy theme analysis helps narrow the artificial gap or lack of integration that sometimes exists between theories of rhetoric and theories of communication.

Bormann (1985) explicates the relationship between "symbolic convergence theory," the generating theoretical construct behind an understanding of rhetorical visions, and fantasy theme criticism, the way readers are able to analyze rhetorical visions. Bormann explains how his study connects humanistic and social scientific perspectives. For example, symbolic convergence theory is quantifiable and offers a basic perspective for the study of communication events (Bormann and Itaba 1992). Fantasy theme analysis, however, is a more critical and qualitative approach to the study of human strategic and reality-constituting discourse. When unified, these two theoretical concepts work toward generating a stronger understanding of both rhetorical and communicative events: they enable each other to work toward a common perspective. As Bormann explains, "The sharing of fantasies within a group or community establishes the assumptive system portrayed in the common rhetorical vision and contributes to the special theory associated with the community's communication style" (1982, 292).

Michael C. McGee concurs with Bormann's assessment and explains how Bormann's theory is an important step in unifying rhetorical and communicative perspectives. He writes, "Bormann's [1972] piece links commonplace arguments in twentieth-century rhetorical and social theory with recent findings in communicology" (1975, 239). Donald C. Shields further indicates the heuristic value of Bormann's contribution to understanding the relationships between interpersonal group dynamics and their larger reality-defining characteristics in the public sphere:

> Whether critiquing American rhetoric, studying group communication, analyzing or managing political campaigns, determining intervention strategies for organizational communication, or developing, assessing, and guiding marketing activities, we have found Bormannean dramatistic theory relevant and beneficial. (1981, 10)

The age of the mass media—in which corporate images become the mind-food of millions of people on a daily basis—accentuates the connections between Bormann's research in interpersonal interactions and larger rhetorical issues of public influence and cultural politics.

The utility of shared fantasies in rhetorical and cultural interactions results from Bales's observation that within zero-history groups (congregations of participants with no prior interaction or localized cultural past), there emerges a *common* culture and group cohesion. The fact that groups of people strive for cohesion is not a particularly significant observation. Because we are social animals who are also symbol-using animals, our social cohesion is necessarily linguistically driven (Burke 1966). What is significant in Bales's research is the *way* in which group cohesion is commonly undertaken. Bales found that shared fantasies, highly structured and ideologically situated symbols, become the currency by which group members negotiate their interpersonal relationships. Over time, these fantasies become more complete and the culture that is created becomes more significant. Thus, these symbols do more than merely bond; they direct people toward specific meanings and thus behaviors. Participants in these fantasies solidify the relationships among themselves via a chain of fantasy themes, that is, an interlocking set of symbols that extends between members. Fantasies, then, are "super-symbols": they symbolize and *justify* at the same time.

These chains of fantasies extend as group members add links. With each link and extension, the fantasy becomes more "real" and its significance becomes increasingly apparent. This reification process continues as more people are brought into the unity of the experience. For example, when Christianity started, it was simply a rhetorical vision that a few people shared. As its various myths and images—its fantasies of death and redemption, divinity and Christhood—chained out among new people who accepted its tenets and added to its "reality" through their assent, Christianity became "real" and achieved a position of cultural dominance in the West. Yet the "realness" of Christianity is not self-evident; its manifest beingness in the world was the result of gradual, not sudden, formulations. The Western world did not become Christian overnight, and it will not remain Christian forever. Christianity became slowly reified over time as it succeeded in supplanting the previous dominant paradigms of Western culture, at which point it grew beyond contention (for a time); the ideology of Christianity became the standard by which its symbols were measured. To challenge Christianity, a person has to work from outside of its symbol system. In its reification, Christianity is complete and is experienced as a "realness" that can be achieved only through an elaborate internalization of its symbols and fantasies. Bormann explains this reification process more fully:

> When group members respond emotionally to the dramatic situation, they publicly proclaim some commitment to an attitude. . . . Dra-

mas also imply motives and by chaining into the fantasy the members gain motivation. Since some of the characters in the fantasies are good people doing laudable things, the group collectively identifies in symbolic terms proper codes of conduct and the characteristics which make people credible message sources. (1972, 397)

Credibility and persuasion are the result of beliefs that people have toward the source of a message, and such credibility is determined, in part, by the position that a source holds in the wider web of belief of a persuadee (Perloff 1993, 145–49). Could not a novel act in the same fashion as a rhetorical text, sanctioning its own symbols by appealing to an ideology that reifies those symbols and authorizes persuaders to speak with a certain range of identifications? Could not a text, like *On the Road*, situate or even create an audience or a "generation" by introducing the symbols and fantasy images of an alternative reality into a social world waiting for a new reality-defining narrative?

Clearly, the answer to the above question is yes. Interpersonal reality-constructing processes become group cohesion processes and, when coupled with the far-reaching influence of the mass media, become rhetorical and public processes by inviting response and commitment. There is no difference in kind between group interactions and cultural interactions; group boundaries become globalized by the mass media that functions to amplify our individuality and merge it into a group or corporate consciousness. The result is, in effect, that the "personal has become political" and that the political has become imagistic (Backman 1991): political thought is largely determined by images. The Sophists of ancient Greece, far from having returned, have never left. Their presence today, however, is more acutely felt now that the guardians of the old order, the Church and the State, have collapsed as icons of natural order (although they remain as conceptual conveniences for many). In the end, the rhetoric of the mass media is controlled by "visionaries." Whether or not these visions are "good" is another matter. As Foucault indicates, "visions" (in the sense that they can be conceived of as "power") are neither "good" nor "bad"; rather, they are "dangerous" (see Swartz 1996b). Consciousness *is* corporate, and this makes the idea of revolt all the more difficult to contemplate.

Bormann addresses the possibility that novels function as a medium for the chaining out of group fantasies when he elaborates upon symbolic convergence theory. Bormann explains that there are three parts to the theory. The first part "deals with the discovery and arrangement of commutative forms and practices into organized and structured patterns that demonstrate the evolution of shared consciousness" (1983, 101). For instance, ideas have histories and these histories are fossilized in discourse and texts. In studying these texts, one can study the evolution of an ideology and its cultural manifestations.[2] As Bernard L. Brock, Robert L. Scott, and James W. Chesebro explain, the first part of symbolic convergence theory "assumes that stable relationships or periods of dynamic equilibrium can be discovered within the complex interactions of human beings and their social and physical context" (1990, 181). One trait of all ideology is that it stabilizes, and this stabilization leaves textual films or residues that can be evaluated.[3]

The second part of symbolic convergence theory, Bormann explains, "consists of a description of the dynamic tendencies within communication systems that explain why the observed practices took place" (1983, 101). Brock, Scott, and Chesebro note:

> If the assumption concerning the degree of social stability is correct, continued work ought to lead toward a critical consensus on a method or set of methods flexible enough to enable the critic to analyze rhetorical patterns typical of the social processes. (1990, 182)

The final part of symbolic convergence theory "consists of the factors that explain why people share the fantasies they do when they do" (Bormann 1983, 101). Bormann elaborates on the importance of this concept:

> Symbolic convergence explains how people come to share enough symbolic ground to take part in logical negotiation processes or to achieve coorientation and also explains how individuals come to share common sentiment or emotional involvement and commitment to symbols. (1983, 102)

The assumptions behind this third dimension of symbolic convergence theory involve the epistemic function of symbols. In discussing this function, Brock, Scott, and Chesebro describe the interplay between language and social reality as "the word-thought-thing relationship" (1990, 182). In this relationship, as in symbolic convergence theory, social reality is created through the communication process by which social communities create meaning. As they explain, specific symbols or combinations of symbols influence human beings and structure their perceptions of reality:

> The word-thought-thing relationship is viewed as reciprocal, that is, not only does the nature of the object (or relationship) affect the selection of words, but the use of a symbol system affects a person's perception of reality. . . . [This] position stresses the dominance of

> the word in the presumed interactions of language and reality as a
> focal point for criticism. (182)

Bormann acknowledges that the significance behind this assumption forms the basic conception of his theory:

> Convergence refers to the way two or more private symbolic worlds
> incline toward each other, come more closely together, or even over-
> lap during certain processes of communication. . . . If several or many
> people develop portions of their private symbolic worlds that over-
> lap as a result of symbolic convergence, they share a common con-
> sciousness and have the basis for communicating with one another
> to create community, to discuss their common experiences, and to
> achieve mutual understanding. (1983, 102)

Accordingly, for fantasy theme critics, shared fantasy becomes the object of study. Fantasy, in this context, has to do with the perception of reality by a rhetor (speaker or writer) in ways that create an alternative explanation for why or how things should be done. When this fantasy is shared, it becomes a drama, and other people behave in ways that support the vision's basic assumptions. When people behave in this manner, they assume positions in the initial vision. In the case of Kerouac, the vision itself became absorbed by the media and exceeded the control of its original source. Social visions often escape their creators and become something larger. When visions become successful, they become nonsummative; they become bigger than the people who create them (see Stewart, Smith, and Denton 1994, 21–22).

In order to uncover the implicit story lines of a fantasy, the reader needs a method of inquiry to bypass the common structure of a word's meaning and to expose the assumptions underlying the communication. In the word-thought-thing relationship, words have only a contingent relationship to the things that they signify. Thus, the "common" structure of word meaning is dependent upon the culture that gives substance to that commonality. As cultural identification becomes localized rather than global, "common" structure gives way to a plurality of narratives, each with its own narrative logic (Fisher 1987). Thus, fantasy theme critics look for a specific narrative logic that substantiates the referent in a rhetorical vision. Toward this end, Roderick P. Hart offers eight "critical probes" that enable the rhetorical reader to "look through message to culture and hence to the roots of persuasion itself" (1990, 306). According to Hart, these questions help one to see "the story lines most often used in a body of discourse and to ask what lessons they teach about people's capacities, about right and wrong, about human purpose" (335).

According to Hart, all rhetorical visions articulate some position with regard to the following:

1. What are the people like?
2. What are the possibilities of group action?
3. Upon what can most people depend?
4. What is human kind's fundamental purpose on earth?
5. What are the fundamental measures of right and wrong?
6. How can success be measured?
7. What sort of information is most dependable?
8. Why do things happen as they do? (336)

Hart's eight questions aid the reader in providing the presuppositions of discourse. For example, when Sal reports that Dean "took all his clothes off, near Ozona, and ran leaping naked in the sage" (1957, 134), Kerouac is expressing a situation in which the reader must infer Dean's ethics. We are being asked, in a sense, to attribute meaning to Dean's actions. Our desire to understand Dean's behavior becomes more pressing when Dean returns to the car where his wife, Marylou, and Sal wait for him and insists that they remove their clothes as well. The passage ends with the three of them, Marylou in the middle, driving naked in a Hudson through Texas. Such a scene may mean different things to different readers, depending upon their moral commitments and sense of good taste. Thus, readers' responses to this passage indicate something about their relationships to the text as well as about their relationships to things in the world outside of the text.

In an effort to understand Dean's actions in this passage, the reader can turn to Hart's fifth question, addressing the issue of "right" and "wrong." This question pays close attention to what Hart calls the "personal ethics" of the character being studied. By comparing an evaluation of Dean in this question with a conception of Dean as revealed though another question, Hart's line of inquiry aids in discovering thematic sources of fantasy types used frequently in a text. For example, the reader can analyze Dean's behavior by incorporating evidence revealed through Hart's second and fifth probes. Together, the observations found in each inquiry reveal Dean's ethical position as influencing the group action by redefining group norms of nakedness. Dean is not simply expressing his own private madness in this scene, or in any other in the book; in fact, Dean is not "doing" anything. "Dean" does not exist; he is a fictional character imagined by Kerouac. Even if the scene in question actually happened, even if Neal Cassady had done what Dean Moriarty does, this point is not diminished. Kerouac is not simply writing about Dean

Moriarty; Dean becomes an expression of an inner freedom and a spiritual dexterity that Kerouac is celebrating. Thus, Dean's actions must be seen against the larger moral backdrop of the novel that calls into question traditional values.

Using Hart's eight questions of inquiry as a way of directing my approach to *On the Road*, I am able to describe plausible plots, myths, and moralizations suggested by Kerouac's rhetoric. The questions serve less as a specific method for research than as a way of organizing my own understanding of the relationship between *On the Road* and the fantasy themes contained therein. In short, they serve as a heuristic that maps the critical road upon which we are about to travel. It may be useful to consider Hart's questions as topological landmarks by which the scenery of the text can be made more familiar. (One final method for exploring the rhetorical dimensions of *On the Road* is incorporated into the approaches designated above: in chapter 8, the concept of liminality is discussed as being the phenomenon from which Kerouac's three fantasy themes arise.)

Disciplinary Critics of Fantasy Theme Analysis

Ten years after the publication of his groundbreaking study, Bormann (1982), in his review of the past decade of research in fantasy theme analysis, reflects on the progress of his theory. In the original study, Bormann claims that a connection exists between the consciousness of a community and the rhetorical visions of its speakers. He hypothesizes that the sharing of collective fantasies is a way that individuals can unite and manipulate their reality. With the hindsight that comes from extensive research, Bormann concludes that his earlier claims are "no longer promising hunches. They have been supported by research results" (289; see also Bormann, Cragan, and Shields 1994).

Not all critics agree with Bormann's enthusiastic assessment of fantasy theme analysis. G. P. Mohrmann, in particular, offers an opposing view. His opposition to the method is primarily articulated in two articles. In the first, which takes place in a colloquy with Bormann, Mohrmann remains "unimpressed" by Bormann's discussion of fantasy theme analysis and the proliferation of studies done with this theory (1982b). The theory itself is dismissed by Mohrmann as "fail[ing] primarily because it is an epideictic exercise" (307). Mohrmann claims that fantasy theme criticism lacks both a "sound rationale" and a "firm intellectual grounding" (310). Furthermore, he writes that "fantasy theme dramas usually are extraordinarily ordinary" (311). These attacks on the dramatistic nature of fantasy theme studies accuse Bormann's method of failing to identify "true dramatic action" and find that characters in the fantasy (heroes and villains) meander through inadequate plots (311). In the second essay, Mohrmann cites an additional problem with the procedure of fantasy theme analysis, namely that the theory "is not a logically consistent extension of the . . . basis from which the writers contend it derives" (1982a, 140). Fundamentally, this argument claims that Bormann misapplied or misinterpreted the conclusion of Bales's 1970s research. Specifically, Mohrmann argues:

> For Bales, fantasy is the product of psychodramatic interaction and is an idiosyncratic reality acting as a temporary buffer against the shock of reality at large. His formulation does not allow the assumption that vestiges of fantasies will appear in the manifest content of other messages, nor does it permit the expectation that other messages have content which will exert direct reciprocal control over later fantasies in small groups. (131)

Bruce E. Gronbeck observes that there are two approaches that readers utilizing fantasy theme analysis take when exploring some phenomenon. By this, Gronbeck means that most fantasy theme studies "seek either to organize a series of events/persons/artifacts . . . or to evaluate actors' social-rhetorical-aesthetic performance within some social setting" (1980, 323). While conclusions drawn on the inductive-analytical level may be problematic when fantasy theme analysis is applied to an extended narrative, such as *On the Road*, the method offers readers an important foothold in the text. Compared to the dynamics and inside jokes of a company staff meeting, the original object of study among many fantasy theme critics, literature has substantially more complex relationships with culture, operating on many levels of individual and national identities. While critics using fantasy theme analysis may make assumptions that do not correspond to the particulars of a specific group, as in Mohrmann's simplistic example of professors spending "psychic income" (1982a), the method can offer an analysis of a more substantial instance of discourse, like a novel, rooted in drama to begin with.

An important distinction must be made between the fantasy theme construct *as* social reality and the fantasy theme construct as being an *indicator* of *a* social reality. Mohrmann's example of professors discussing their psychic income is presented with the assumption that "[t]he posture is clearly etched. A fantasy theme drama *is* social reality" (1982a, 122, emphasis added). Bormann clarifies the position of the fantasy theme critic. He argues, "The fantasy theme drama *when shared* is a key to the social reality. It is not by itself the social reality" (1982, 304). Mohrmann is correct in his feeling that cause and effect relationships cannot be predicted using fantasy theme analysis, but Bormann never makes this claim. Bormann simply suggests that the fantasy theme critic can explore communicative tendencies among members of a social group. Gronbeck elaborates on the general problems with fantasy theme analysis:

> It has been suspect for its Freudian base, for its post hoc character (meaning that almost anything can be explained by it at least analogically), for its systematic development of private vocabulary (especially the theme/type/vision trilogy), for the difficulty in identifying the chaining process when dealing with society-wide events, and for its tendency toward subjectivistic treatments of themes and types. (1980, 324)

Unlike some critics, however, Gronbeck does conclude his criticism of fantasy theme analysis on a positive note by declaring that "its popularity as a critical method cannot be doubted: its very elasticity, while a vice to some, is also a virtue, for it presumably can treat seriously any discourse relying principally on narratives" (324). Gronbeck highlights what I consider to be the main defense of the theory: the ability of the fantasy theme critic to detect communicative patterns implicit in a narrative that suggest basic assumptions grounding the rhetor-audience reality.

Edwin Black develops the position of the above critics when he explains that

> fantasy theme analysis, by anticipating prior to inspection the course of a belief, and by imposing on all of its subjects a categorical scheme that is reductive in its power of description, sometimes has yielded criticism that seems formulary and predictable. (1980, 335)

Furthermore, Black argues, the "etic" approach to conducting rhetorical criticism often views "a rhetorical transaction in terms of a pre-existing theoretical formulation" (333). Black draws upon the "etic" and "emic" polarity from Kenneth L. Pike's *Language in Relation to a Unified Theory of the Structure of Human Behavior* (1967). Pike explains this distinction more fully: "The etic viewpoint studies behavior as from outside of a particular system, and as an essential initial approach to an alien system. The emic viewpoint results from studying behavior as from inside the system" (37). The etic approach to criticism involves an important bias that must be addressed. Specifically, as Black notes, "A problem of applying any pre-existing theory to the interpretation of a rhetorical transaction is that the critic is disposed to find exactly what he or she expected to find." Consequently, "[S]uch criticism tends much more to be a confirmation than an inquiry" (1980, 333), though in countering

Black, I would point out that confirmation does not necessarily exclude inquiry, since there is a difference between finding what is expected and exploring and understanding the elements of some context. Black, however, argues that the theory itself is secondary to the psychological processes that it attempts to embrace in the domain of rhetoric:

> [A] rhetorical theory may be grounded in a view of the psychological regularities that bear upon rhetorical transitions, as fantasy theme analysis purports to be. . . . But inasmuch as rhetorical transactions are themselves a major source of information about such psychological regularities—and about situational regularities as well—it seems as though criticism would stand much more to inform this sort of rhetorical theory than to be informed by it. (333)

In the exploration of a text, the intuition of a reader, guided perhaps by preconceived notions, can direct inquiry that reveals important findings. These findings may even discredit the initial assumption that the reader might hold. The obligation of the investigator is to deal honestly with the situation and to adjust for discrepancies. In terms of my study, I did anticipate finding fantasy themes in *On the Road*, but I was unsure of what exactly I would find and surprised by the extent to which I found the themes. What is more, in the case of *On the Road*, I found that casual conversation with those who had read and were affected by the book testifies to the premise that the novel is powerful in its ability to influence people's lives. Time and again, I heard the response that the book had caused readers to drop out of school, quit their jobs, and move to the West. The question that is raised for the critic is, "How?" This study is one attempt to answer that question.

Another specific area of concern with fantasy theme criticism involves the generalizability of an acknowledged rhetorical vision to the population of individuals purported to be affected by that vision. In other words, are rhetorical visions as powerful on the level of the individual as my study of *On the Road* suggests? McGee, for instance, reminds us that a study of rhetorical visions (or "myths" as he calls them) cannot provide a complete explanation of social behavior:

> Typically "the people" justify political philosophies; their only concrete significance is their existence, for not even their identity is agreed upon by those who appeal to them. About the only point of agreement is that, in politics, "the people" are omnipotent; they are an idea of collective force which transcends both individuality and reason. (1975, 238)

Bormann agrees that there is an emotional component to McGee's "myth." Consequently, he makes it evident that group identity is not nearly as important as dramatic confrontations between individuals who perceive themselves as accepting of a particular group idea. As he explains:

> The fantasizing is accompanied by emotional arousal; the dreams embodied in the fantasies drive participants towards actions and efforts to achieve them; the sharing of fantasies provides a social reality peopled by anthropomorphic forces and imagined and historical personages in dramatic confrontation. (1985, 9)

Bormann goes on to explain that the creation of a social reality is individualistic and rises through a rhetorical process as people interpret the communicative world around them. Rhetoric, according to Bormann, is not "the only modality that people use in epistemic fashion to generate social knowledge and reality, but I do claim it is a major means to that end" (1982, 304). When a novel is thought of as rhetorical discourse, its analysis fits Bormann's assumptions.[4]

In opposition to the importance Bormann places on the dramatization of social fantasies, Mohrmann vehemently argues that fantasy theme criticism is an "epideictic" exercise and that it is "unstimulating." Moreover, Mohrmann accuses Bormann of falsely interpreting some of the basic presumptions of Bales's original work. Bormann counters this charge by separating himself from both Bales and a Freudian influence: "My answer is that the only thing for which we are indebted to Bales is his finding of the dynamic process of sharing group fantasies. . . . However, we have departed from those who have followed Bales' lead into psychohistory" (1982, 303).

Mohrmann's polemic continues. He writes, "I am convinced that the ground of argument is encumbered rather than clarified when all the old critical vocabulary is collapsed into 'fantasy themes' and 'rhetorical vision,' [and] the whole is encompassed in dramatism." Moreover, he exclaims, "since fantasy theme critics wall everything in and nothing out, many do treat topics far removed from traditional concerns and vocabulary" of the rhetorical critic. With a significant degree of understatement, Mohrmann adds to his position, "I admit to a marked dissatisfaction with the theoretical basis Bormann uses in his program for criticism" (1980, 270).

Charles E. Williams elaborates on Mohrmann's concerns. He points out that Mohrmann "has linked fantasy theme analysis to a hobby horse that apparently generates a lot of interest but takes the rider, in this case the critic, absolutely nowhere" (1987, 11). Is this statement a valid criticism of the rhetorical vision methodology? In order to assess the truth or falsity of this assertion, it is important to evaluate the three fantasy visions that I have isolated and named in this study.

First, as I demonstrate in chapter 5, Kerouac's rhetorical influence derives, in part, from a vision and glorification of social deviance. In recognizing unbridled experience as the manna of a person's soul—as the truth standard for human existence—Kerouac positions his readers to understand social deviance as both desirable and a spiritual duty. Social deviance becomes a religious aspiration; any resistance to a static existence becomes a holy quest. The "Vision of Sexuality" (chapter 6) is the second fantasy theme manifested in the text. This vision locates social deviance in the libido and gives Beat culture its distinctly phallocentric tone. The third fantasy theme, "Dean as Vision" (chapter 7), gives agency to *On the Road*'s overarching rhetorical themes by personifying Kerouac's secularized divine spirit in Dean Moriarty. All three visions are rhizomatically interdependent—they touch upon each other and interact, constructing multiple layers of meaning and influence. In fleshing out these meanings, and in situating them in their sociological and historical contexts, the reader gains a greater understanding of the rhetorical impulses of persuaders in the cultural realms, countering Mohrmann's objection that the method is worthless.

In isolating three fantasy themes, I have named *On the Road* as the clearest expression of Kerouac's rhetorical vision. On the basis of this evidence—my analysis of the text, my stipulation of its rhetorical structure—I contribute to an understanding of the rhetoric of a social community. Bormann substantiates my claim that community consciousness is rhetorically situated and that narrative is the means by which consciousness takes its form. He explains that a critical commitment to elucidating fantasy themes is heuristic because it leads to a thorough comprehension of a culture and reveals meaning as negotiated between text and context:

> A viable rhetorical vision must accommodate the community to the changes that accompany its unfolding history. The rhetoric must deal with the anxieties aroused by times of trouble, by the evil defined within the social reality. The rhetoric must deal with the changing circumstances and social conflict. Communication is the means by which the community makes and implements plans and interprets its success and failure. In much of the functioning rhetoric, therefore, problem-solving communication, argument, logic, evidence, proof, and refutation play a prominent part. The question remains: What is the relationship between shared fantasies and logical proofs or good reasons? (1982, 292)

To answer Bormann's question, fantasies offer the recipient an alternative system of logic and morality. Specifically, *On the Road* represents a long argument in the form of a narrative that provides examples of pathetic proof that are acceptable only to individuals who have internalized the chaining-out process of the implicit fantasy themes.

As the critics of fantasy theme analysis note, limitations exist with the procedure. For example, a problem with qualitative research is that precious few precautions are taken against investigator bias. To adjust for the tensions between epideictic exercise and "objectivity," I made substantial effort to keep this study on the argumentative level as opposed to the selectively celebrative level. A further limitation is that the criticism involves a single analysis. Ideally, other critics will study the same text and, in the interchange of our different analyses, be able to flesh out a deeper meaning and structural appeal in Kerouac's work. In addition, focusing almost exclusively on *On the Road* narrows my claims about Kerouac's overall vision. Accentuating this limitation is the fact that hundreds of other texts in the Beat and countercultural literatures have been ignored. Effort in the future can be made to collaborate my findings with the visions contained, and perhaps duplicated, in other works written under Kerouac's shadow.

Supplementary Theorists

In an effort to fortify the theoretical foundations of this study, I have supplemented Bormann's theory with the work of Roderick P. Hart (1990), Michael C. McGee (1975), and Maurice Charland (1987). Hart circumnavigates some of the problems identified with Bormann's development of fantasy theme criticism. He takes "some license . . . in order to make the construct immediately useful to the critic" (1990, 329). In his chapter on cultural analysis, Hart examines how culture becomes embedded in language. For the cultural critic, three areas of union between culture and language are of utmost importance: values, myths, and fantasy themes. The three "almost always work together," Hart explains (305). Furthermore, Hart elaborates on Bormann by explaining that "fantasy themes are *fantasies* because they point to an idealized world and *themes* because they are popular, repeated understandings of what such a world is, was, or will be" (306). For Hart, fantasy themes "are mythic shorthand, story lines describing an idealized (but not necessarily ideal) past, present, or future" (329).

McGee adds a new dimension to Bormann's theory by discussing political "myths" and their effect on mass social movements. In my study of Kerouac, McGee's conceptualization of "myth" and "the people," as rhetorical ontology, are hereafter used interchangeably with Bormann's notion of rhetorical vision. McGee offers justification for regarding the two theories as functionally similar:

> Stated simply, the problem is this: How can one combine the idea of "people" in a way which accounts for the rhetorical function of "the people" in argument designed to warrant social action, even society itself? . . . Bormann believes that such concepts as "The People" may be strictly linguistic phenomena introduced into public argument as a means of "legitimizing" a collective fantasy. The advocate, he suggests, dangles a dramatic vision of the people before his audience. The audience, essentially a group of individuals, reacts with a desire to participate in that dramatic vision, to become "the people" described by the advocate. (1975, 240)

Specifically, McGee elaborates on the rhetorical construct of "the people":

> "The people" . . . are not objectively real in the sense that they exist as a collective entity in nature; rather, they are a fiction dreamed by an advocate and infused with an artificial, rhetorical reality by the agreement of an audience to participate in a collective fantasy. (240)

According to McGee, myths influence and transform "generations." Fundamental to my study of Kerouac is McGee's sentiment that "[a]s myths change, 'generations' change, and with the new 'generation' comes a new 'people,' defined not by circumstance or behavior, but by their collective faith in a rhetorical vision" (246).

In extending McGee's work, Charland discusses how the socialization process of fantasy, with its qualities of identification, is intrinsic to the narrative. He explains how "[n]arratives 'make real' coherent subjects. They constitute subjects as they present a particular textual position. . . . [N]arratives offer a world in which human agency is possible and acts can be meaningful" (1987, 139). Within the context of a narrative, identification and socialization take place. Within the socialization process, "identity defines inherent motives and interests that a rhetoric can appeal to" (137). In a social movement, this is a long-term process: the "rhetoric of identification is ongoing, not restricted to one hailing, but usually part of the rhetoric of socialization" (138).

While socialization implies a bringing together, it also implies a taking apart, a disintegration of another social network (Burke 1969b, 25). With this in mind, I have used John Waite Bowers and Donovan J. Ochs to augment fantasy theme analysis. These authors provide material for understanding the role social deviance has among groups struggling to articulate their visions of "reality." Insights gained from their approach are incorporated into the larger perspective created by the fantasy theme method. Bowers and Ochs provide a study that, like the prior studies, concerns itself with social change. Bowers and Ochs explain that their study is a "handbook . . . designed to provide the basis for understanding the instrumental and symbolic acts performed in the service of agitation and control" (1971, preface). Their description of agitation is most helpful for this study of Kerouac: "We say that agitation exists . . . when a movement for significant social change from outside the establishment meets such resistance within the establishment that more than the normal discursive means of persuasion occur" (1971, 6). As will become clear in the next chapter, *On the Road* is a book that is intimately concerned with social agitation; it is a testimony to the will of the human spirit to resist control.

Part Two
View from the Road

5

The Vision of Social Deviance

Kerouac's "path" is laid out in his fiction, most popularly in *On the Road*, and is represented in three predominant rhetorical visions: the Vision of Social Deviance, the Vision of Sexuality, and Dean as Vision. Each vision serves as a general base supporting the next vision in a pyramid form. The primary vision that grounds the bulk of the narrative has to do with the rejection of popular culture; this I call the Vision of Social Deviance.

On the Road begins with the narrator's immediate rejection of the world that American culture has to offer him. "I first met Dean not long after my wife and I split up" (1957, 5), begins Sal Paradise, a young, noncommitted college student surviving on the G.I. Bill. We meet Sal after he has just gotten over "a serious illness . . . that had something to do with the miserably weary split-up and [my] feeling that everything was dead" (1957, 5). We are never told what this illness is, and there is never any further reference to Sal's former wife. The past is clouded in mystery.

Sal reveals that the "split" was "miserably weary." Was this a divorce? A separation? Was this a long marriage that left the pair emotionally distraught? Did Sal leave his wife? Did Sal's wife leave him? We are not given any details. We are not even sure what "miserably weary" means. While the context is not clear, the tone is: Sal feels as if everything is dead. Even so, the careful reader has reasons to interrogate the text further—this is especially true for the reader who blurs the distinction between fiction and nonfiction, as well as one who realizes that Kerouac made little effort to hide the fact that his "fiction" was largely autobiographical.

In real life, Kerouac met Neal Cassady in December 1946. Kerouac had married Edie Parker in August 1944 but left her in October (they were divorced later after attempts at reconciliation). Parker was connected to Kerouac's arrest as a material witness and accomplice after the fact to Lucien Carr's killing of Dave Kammerer. To raise money for bail, Parker's family lawyer insisted that Kerouac marry Edie (Nicosia 1994, 129). Under these marital conditions, it is difficult to imagine that the split would have been "miserably weary." Thus, Sal's narrative, although not necessarily biographically accurate in terms of Kerouac's life, is textually significant. The book *begins* with the element of death. The larger narrative that follows becomes, by extension, an after-death experience or, more neoreligiously, a rebirth. Thus, from the first lines of the text, Kerouac positions the reader for a major transformation.

Death, disease, and weariness characterize the old world from which Kerouac has moved away. The new world, suggested but not articulated at this point in the text, promises something else. More than a new beginning, the text promises a new life, literally. Even the name that Kerouac chose for his persona is suggestive of this experience of rebirth. "Sal" is etymologically related to Paul (originally named Saul), a chief persecutor of Christ's followers who changed his axiology and his identity and became an important herald of the gospel.[1] "Paradise" is the state or condition of the reborn soul in Christian mythology. Both Sal and Paul experience a spiritual death at the beginning of their narratives, and both are transformed by the coming of a new cultural order. Seen in another way, the social institutions of marriage, formal education, and the military failed to supply Paradise with the energy and self-fulfillment that his soul desired. These three institutions, along with work and traditional religion, are the cornerstones of American culture and are widely rejected in the text.

The book's opening sentence presents two important rhetorical breaks from prior literary tradition and infuses in the reader the volatility of Sal's not-quite-so-unique predicament. First, Sal's declaration of discontent breaks from "literature as entertainment to writing as a necessary mode of expressing a particular vision" (Tytell 1976, 70). In other words, Kerouac's style warns the reader that something different is going to happen in the text; the opening tone is a flag that prepares the reader for a different type of reading experience.[2] The effect of this new style is captivating. Bruce Cook explains what happened to him when he first read *On the Road*:

> That started it for me. I soon came to regard the Beats as my generation. I felt the same keen sense of identification with them that

thousands of others my age did, and I had the same feeling that I was lucky to be in on the beginning of something big. (1971, 3)

That "something big" was a new life, a life that could only be appreciated once people understood that the old life was "dead," at least symbolically. People may have felt that something was wrong with American culture, as discontent existed prior to its naming in *On the Road*. Yet the situation had not been named, at least for middle-class white America, as Kerouac named it by positioning the life that his book documents against the death and the cultural void present and transcended in the opening paragraph.

Extending from the first, the second rhetorical break is evident in the opening sentiment. After shifting from "literature as entertainment" toward "literature as equipment for living," and after contrasting the death and weariness of the old with the promise of something better in the new vision of the world that Kerouac is offering, Kerouac implicitly does something else: he effectively offers an empathetic lure into the hungry cultural waters of young readers who "felt trapped in the bind of societal or parental expectations, bound by the ethos of personal secrecy and self-confinement" (Tytell 1976, 160). This was an age of loyalty: to parents, to country, to God. Each of these loyalties placed demands on young people and forced them to think and feel in certain ways.

The 1950s were a time of suspicion, as exemplified in loyalty oaths and expectations of obedience (Lamont 1990). As the United States government was preparing its citizens for a stultifying Cold War mentality, anything that was considered different was immediately suspect. This was a time when the government provoked fears of Communism and instigated mass witch hunts that condemned many Americans for their legitimate and constitutionally protected actions on behalf of the American political Left (Klehr and Haynes 1992). This culture of suspicion is exemplified in the 1956 Allied Artists film *Invasion of the Body Snatchers*, based on the book by Jack Finney (1955). While the film is ostensibly about space aliens who take over people's bodies in an attempt to control the world, it is, in effect, an anti-Communist film that helped to cultivate an atmosphere of fear (Johnson 1979).

In the film, the "good" characters (red-blooded Americans) can never tell who is or who is not an alien. The aliens *look* like everyone else, but there is something sinister about them, something cold, calculating, ruthless. Likewise, "good" people in the real world of Cold War politics can never tell for sure who is or who is not a Communist. The aliens are analogous to the Communists, who are just as sinister, according to the official propaganda of the United States. As De Villo Sloan explains:

> To be recruited into [the aliens'] ranks is to join the legions of the living dead. When Benell [the hero of the narrative] encounters [the aliens] at the end of the narrative, they calmly try to reason with him, describing a utopian vision of the future, if only all humans would join them. At this juncture, the discourse is political. It easily conjures up images of Marxist utopians, possible only if the self is given up to the collective. (1988, 185)

Films such as *Invasion of the Body Snatchers* accentuated a fear of Communism in the American public and, by extension, a fear of any social idea that was "left of center." As Glen M. Johnson explains:

> No one can be trusted: the plot of *The Body Snatchers* develops thorough an accumulation of paranoid denunciations of familiars—niece accuses uncle, wife accuses husband, students accuse teacher, son accuses mother. The political parallel is inescapable. "Remember, always," J. Edgar Hoover wrote in *Masters of Deceit*, "that there are thousands of people in this country now working in secret to make it happen here." (1979, 6)

Thus, Hollywood played (as it continues to play) an important role in providing the U.S. government with ideological weapons to justify the arms expenditures that were necessary for it to run its colonies during the Cold War (as well as its current client-states) and to reify the consciousness of consumerism (Bird 1989; Fyne 1985; Parenti 1992; and Smoodin 1988).

As the above suggests, 1950s America was a culture in which any deviance was considered *moral* deviance and was deemed a threat. This threat was not just political. John Tytell highlights the rhetorical atmosphere embedded deeply in the puritanical roots of this country and the concomitant notion that "one's inner being was really suspect, a source of embarrassment or liability, shame or incrimination" (1976, 160). This suspicion, in many ways, was sexual, but it was more than that; any reduction of 1950s conservatism to sexual repression is an oversimplification. Rather, suspicion was based on an irrational fear that was deliberately and rationally presented by the United States government in order to manipulate the American public (Herman and Chomsky 1988; Chomsky 1989; Carey 1997). U.S. propaganda constantly maintained that the American way of life was about to end, that it was menaced on multiple fronts, and that plurality itself was its greatest threat.[3] To guard the United States against this danger, the social/cultural realm was closely policed by agents of the status quo.

The agitation of Kerouac's rhetorical fantasy struck against the above sentiments and prevailing consciousness, contributed to the identity of a subculture, and cracked the wall of cold mores that was bound eventually to crumble. *On the Road* is a call for plurality; it rejects the culture of suspicion and control. It is not pro-Communist or pro-Socialist, but it is not anti-Communist or anti-Socialist either. Rather, it is pro-body, pro-desire, pro-experience—similar in many ways to the Left politics found in the writings of such social theorists as Gilles Deleuze and Felix Guattari (for example, 1983).[4] Kerouac sees through the propaganda of anti-Communism and asks difficult questions about what it means to be an "American." The book takes us through all parts and experiences of American society—the dirty, the dark, the alternative rationalities and potentialities, things that were formally alien to Kerouac's middle-class reading public.

Cook, for instance, notes the effect *On the Road* had at the time of its publication: "There was a sort of instantaneous flash of recognition that seemed to send thousands of [youth] out into the streets, proclaiming that Kerouac had written their story" (1971, 7). These were the children of the middle class, and they identified with the book so immensely because it broadened their experiences and suggested something more than the limited and limiting messages that they were receiving from their parents, churches, and government, all of which were busy encouraging them to think in politically safe ways. Similar to Sal, they were struggling with their sense of feeling dead. Ironically, these children felt the *inverse* of what movies such as *Invasion of the Body Snatchers* were trying to establish. It became increasingly clear to those who felt alienated from the traditional notions of American culture that the "real" zombies were not the "indoctrinated" citizens of Communist countries but were the American people themselves. The threat to U.S. freedom was not the Soviet Union or the American Communist party, but rather the state religion of anti-Communism and other social pressures that gave the Church and State a tyrannical power over the lives of many young people. This is not an entirely new observation. In 1944, Albert Camus was able to give public support to the claim that "[a]nticommunism is the beginning of dictatorship" (1991, 59).

To the alienated youth of America, Kerouac provides an alternative. Striking out against the death and deprivation of his era, Kerouac, in the third sentence of the novel, introduces Dean Moriarty as the catalyst of his salvation. From beyond the cultural grave, the persona of the narrator speaks out, guided by the shining light of rebirth. Immediately, the reader senses this shift from death to life as Moriarty appears in the text, evoking Kerouac's vision as well as Sal's spiritual redemption. Sal muses, "With the coming of Dean Moriarty began the part of my life you could call my life on the road" (1957, 5). With Moriarty, the reader is introduced to a critical change in perspective. Sal's narrative is about being on the road. But what is so special about the *road* that it becomes the central motif of the novel? For an overt answer to this question, the reader has to wait, although there are clues early in the novel that suggest the "true" value of Kerouac's road. Simply, "the road is life" (1957, 175), Kerouac explains. In Kerouac's world, the road leads away from his symbolic death in the city—the world of work, marriage, school, and the military. Dean is the prophet of the road because he is able to teach others the true metaphysical significance of the road. Sal comments that "Dean is the perfect guy for the road because he actually was born on the road, when his parents were passing through Salt Lake City in 1926, in a jalopy, on their way to Los Angeles" (1957, 5).

The road takes Kerouac from the spiritual poverty of traditional American life. The road, stretching across the breadth of this nation, becomes the symbol of America's true wealth and potential. Kerouac's road is literal; it is the highway to the West, the old Oregon Trail by which the dispossessed and the hopeless could travel in search of a new life. But the road is much more than that; it is the symbolic expression of all spiritual "roads"—it is the dharma path made manifest in asphalt. Since the road is as much spiritual as it is physical, Kerouac needs a spiritual as well as a physical guide. When Kerouac writes that he is going "on the road," he does not mean that he is driving to St. Louis. Destinations are not important. Rather, the "road" represents an odyssey; it itself is a drama. In other words, the "road" is a wilderness; it is *not* the most direct path between two cities. This is why Dean Moriarty is such an important figure in the text and in Kerouac's world. Dean is not simply the companion figure to Sal in the novel, the "other" to Sal's observations. Dean *is* the novel. Sal could spend his entire life traveling across the country, but without Dean, that travel could not be a transcendence. Likewise, people traveled before Kerouac wrote *On the Road*, but such travel often became a transcendent experience for those who had read the book.[5]

Dean literally is the spirit of the text, just as Neal Cassady is the spirit of the counterculture. Dean/Neal is also the driver of the cars in which Sal/Kerouac sometimes travels. It is ironic, but it also makes sense when considering the above, that Kerouac never got a driver's license—Kerouac is not the driving force of his own vision. Kerouac simply amplifies the vision that he finds embodied in Neal. Or perhaps both visions are symbiotic: Kerouac's vision, embodied in Neal, helps define Neal, and Neal, in turn, gives Kerouac a concrete set of values to amplify and celebrate. Either way, in *On the Road*, it is Dean, not Sal, who is the outcast prophet through whom the road becomes meaningful, becomes something more than a path between two cities. Dean's spirit is the backdrop upon which the drama of the road can be witnessed. In short, Dean Moriarty is the incarnate soul of the deity Paradise witnesses while passing through the great Western desert: "As we crossed the Colorado-Utah border I saw God in the sky in the form of huge gold sunburning clouds above the desert that seemed to point a finger at me and say, 'Pass here and go on, you're on the road to heaven'" (1957, 150).

Prior to meeting Moriarty, Paradise was drawn to the allure of the road and planned to travel, yet he never actualized those plans due to what we can assume to be the responsibilities of the systemic world: the world of marriage, work, and school. Sal's opening comments emphasize the fundamental antithesis between the vision Paradise is breaking from and the one that he is working toward. The friction that Sal feels as he contemplates moving from one worldview to another is the result of a conflict in values between the two structures. The actual process of Sal's shifting between two worldviews affects his life perspective. We can gain a clearer understanding of the importance of this change in Sal's development by applying John Waite Bowers and Donovan J. Ochs's discussion of lateral and vertical deviance to the text (1971).

For Bowers and Ochs, vertical deviance (or "agitation") involves discontent *within* a value system. An example of this involves workers who strike for higher wages, more time off, better working conditions, and improved health privileges, but who do not fundamentally disagree with the business institution itself or the economic culture of society at large. The questioning, in this instance, is not of the value system behind the economics of the community. The system remains intact; dissenters question effects of those values in their lives but do not attack the values themselves. Such a position is not revolutionary: it is an attempt to get the system to reconcile itself to its own meanings, potentialities, and promises.

The above is the position of "agitation" as it is represented by the official rhetoric of this country. For propagandistic reasons, the government often subsumes social unrest by co-opting it and making it appear as if the system is voluntarily working for dissenters. This sentiment is exemplified in Bill Clinton's first inaugural address when he emphatically states, "There is nothing wrong with America that cannot be cured by what is right with America" (1993, 75). Clinton, as a representative of U.S. liberalism, recognizes that there are problems in America but denies that the problems have systemic roots, thus cutting off the possibility for institutional change. Considering that Clinton is the president, his rhetoric is understandable: he co-opts dissent by recognizing it and diffusing its challenge to fundamental American economic practices. In the typology of political positions, this is a "progressive" position (Rossiter 1962). Yet such progressivism is not confrontational; both parties in the dispute are working from the same fundamental vision. The question becomes, How will their differences be managed? (Cathcart 1978, 237–38). This is a reformist position, characteristic of American liberalism that transcends the peculiarities of the two Clinton administrations.

Sal had been working from a vertical position of discontent prior to meeting Dean. Along with millions of other Americans, Paradise was able to divorce his wife, reject the authority of the armed services, work haphazardly toward a college education, and engage in a succession of part-time and temporary jobs, all without directly questioning the values behind these institutions. In other words, Paradise was unhappy with his life and his world but could not see the cause of his problems as being systemic to the dominant culture that had no place for him. In traditional Marxist terms, people such as Sal are suffering from ideology—a false consciousness that is imposed on them by the hegemonic social order (Eagleton 1991). According to this position, the disenfranchised, the poor, and the masses of the lower working classes and unemployed have every reason to rebel against the social order that impoverishes them. The fact that they do not rebel and instead have their revolutionary consciousness thwarted by television, racism, sexism, and other tantalizing candies dangled in front of them is the result and function of ideology.[6]

Paradise clearly desired to be outside of the institutions that forced their hold on him, clearly struggled for a new life, but in vain. All he could experience, all he could *hope* to experience given the epistemology (or ideology) that he was subject to, led him to a miserable state of weariness and despair. The structural condition of Sal's predicament can be understood better in Roland Barthes's terms:

> For the very end of myths is to immobilize the world: they must suggest and mimic a universal order which has fixated once and for all the hierarchy of possession. Thus, every day and everywhere, man is stopped by myths, referred by them to this motionless prototype which lives in his place, stifles him in the manner of a huge internal parasite and assigns to his activity the narrow limits within which he is allowed to suffer without upsetting the world. (1972, 155)

In short, Sal lacked the direction and insight to be able to break from his past (that is, to "upset the world") and to gain agency and influence over his future. His initial attempts to escape from his old life were ruinous: he was still trapped in the value system that the situations of work and family represent, and this powerless feeling led Paradise to the perception of death and disease in his static existence. Sal had reached a point at which he could go no farther, and his vertical perspective prevented him from actually dropping out and taking to the road, which would have been a transformation into lateral agitation. This sentiment is evident in the line "I'd often dream of going West to see the country, always vaguely planning and never taking off" (1957, 5).

As evidenced above, the first page of the novel is where we find a stunted, disgruntled, and symbolically dead Sal, a man who could not find peace with himself or with the world, a man in need of a cultural space in which to transform (as a caterpillar needs a specific space to transform into a butterfly). With his relationship to Dean, that space opens up, as if Dean's presence has the power to reorder physical as well as conceptual space. Life begins to change for Sal. Sal undergoes a metamorphosis—and it is here that the "text" begins.

Obviously, the first page is the beginning of the book in a chronological sense. More importantly, however, we can say that the book conceptually begins in its first paragraph rather than somewhere deep in its body, as is the case with many novels. In contrast, we can also say that the book does not start in the first sentence, as the first sentence is narrated by a dead man. Another way to get at the same idea is to explain how the book conceptually begins with Sal's metamorphosis—his change from a position of vertical agitation to one of lateral agitation. Bowers and Ochs explain that "[a]gitation based on lateral deviance occurs when the agitators dispute the value system itself" (1971, 7). With that change in Sal, our entire perspective with regard to the text changes.

One of among many passages illustrates the effect that Dean has on Sal:

> I had been spending a quiet Christmas in the country, as I realized when we got back into the house and I saw the Christmas tree, the presents, and smelled the roasting turkey and listened to the talk of the relatives, but now the bug was on me again, and the bug's name was Dean Moriarty, and I was off on another spur around the road. (1957, 96)

This new perspective is reinforced throughout the book and questions the value system of American institutions. A passage from *Visions of Cody* clearly illustrates that Kerouac, having made the break in his personal life, is writing from a point of lateral agitation:

> In America, the idea of going to college is just like the idea of prosperity is just around the corner, this is supposed to solve something or everything . . . because all you had to do was larn [sic] what they taught and then everything else was going to be handled; instead of that, and just like prosperity that was never around the corner but a couple of miles at least (and false prosperity—) going to college by acquainting me with all the mad elements of life, such as the sensibilities, books, arts, histories of madness, and fashions, has not only made it impossible for me to learn simple tricks of how to earn a living but has deprived me of my one-time innocent belief in my own thoughts that used to make me handle my own destiny. (1972, 259)

This is a particularly cogent passage. In it, Kerouac is more than a disgruntled or frustrated student; he is more than a college "dropout." Kerouac does not fail in school; rather, he comes to recognize that school *is part of the problem.* School, like so many other systemic pressures, prevents Kerouac from handling his "own destiny." But the passage is about more than destiny: it is about lying, illusions, false pretense; it is about a game that most people are made to play and a value system based upon a myth. Kerouac reinterprets the dominant myths that guide our middle-class culture and stakes his personal existence in direct opposition to it.

Kerouac's questioning in the above passage is exemplified in the persona of Dean. Dean is not school-educated like Sal, and this is one of his strengths. Unlike Sal, who is "deprived" of his "innocent" thoughts that helped him to handle his own destiny, Dean does nothing else but live out his destiny. Throughout the book, Dean is also portrayed as "innocent"—his crimes and transgressions are always "angelic" because Dean lives in "time," in "destiny," in "truth." Dean is free while the rest of us suffer through formal educations that enslave us to the decrepit morality that Kerouac fears. Dean's education is from the university of life where he "spent a third of his time in the pool hall, a third in jail, and a third in the public library" (1957, 8).

As the mechanism for Sal's transformation, Dean's life becomes an extension, a manifest form of Sal's innate questioning. From the outset of the book, Sal strives for a complete spiritual identification with Dean. However, by the end of the book, when Sal sits on the broken-down pier in New Jersey and muses about Dean's missing father, there is a sense in which Sal has failed to maintain the intensity of that identification. Dean's father remains Dean's father; he does not become "our" father. Sal and Dean are clearly separate, but this does not matter. Identification is never complete as Dean is too intense and too holy for Sal to achieve total consubstantiality with him. The questioning itself ultimately becomes a powerful form of social agitation. As Gregory Stephenson explains, "For Sal, Dean represents a psychological and spiritual reorientation, a new pattern of conduct, a new system of values, including spontaneity, sensuality, energy, intuition, and instinct" (1990, 156).

Bowers and Ochs discuss social agitation as occurring "when a group has a grievance or grievances" and no alleviation is built into the existing social structure (1971, 7). These theorists define agitation as the state in which "people outside the normal decision making establishment . . . advocate a significant social change and . . . encounter a degree of resistance within the establishment" (4). By this definition, Sal's opening lines and Kerouac's distinct tone in *On the Road* qualify as instances of agitation. But why, for what reason, and for and against whom?

On one level Kerouac, through Paradise, is striving to create for himself a situation of freedom and experience by rejecting as insufficient the value base offered to him by his culture. The values of this culture and its moral deficiencies are mocked by Sal and Dean when they arrive in Washington during President Truman's second inauguration. They encounter, on Pennsylvania Avenue, "Great displays of war might . . .B-29's, PT boats, artillery, all kinds of war material that looked murderous in the snowy grass; the last thing was a regular small ordinary lifeboat that looked pitiful and foolish." Dean's reply to all this is, "What are these people up to? Harry's sleeping somewhere in this town. . . . Good old Harry. . . . Man from Missouri, as I am. . . . That must be his own boat" (1957, 112). However, their discontent with the dominant values of this society soon changes from naive mockery to a more soul-grating realization of what the values of their rejected culture have held for the peoples of the Earth. Here Paradise describes a meeting with some Indians of the Sierra Madre:

> [The Indians] watched Dean, serious and insane at his raving wheel, with eyes of hawks. All had their hands outstretched. They had come down from the back of mountains and higher places to hold forth their hands for something they thought civilization could offer, and they never dreamed the sadness and the poor broken delusion of it. They didn't know that a bomb had come that could crack all our bridges and roads and reduce them to jumbles, and we could be as poor as they someday, and stretching out our hands in the same, same way. (1957, 24)

The inability of materialism to provide for the spiritual/cultural needs of Americans becomes obvious when Kerouac writes of the above scene in *Visions of Cody*: "All the Indians along the road want something from us. We wouldn't be on the road if we had it" (1972, 380).

Kerouac's discontent with American capitalism and its destructive qualities is more bluntly communicated by Bull, another character in *On the Road*, modeled after William S. Burroughs. Bull exclaims, "The bastards right now are only interested in seeing if they can blow up the world" (1957, 128). Bull continues his condemnation of the establishment's consciousness:

> "These bastards have invented plastics by which they could make houses that last forever. And tires. Americans are killing themselves by the millions every year with defective rubber tires that get hot on the road and blow up. They could make tires that never blow up. Same with tooth powder. There's a certain gum they've invented and they won't show it to anybody that if you chew it as a kid you'll never

get a cavity for the rest of your born days. Same with clothes. They can make clothes that last forever. They prefer making cheap goods so's everybody have to go on working and punching timeclocks and organizing themselves in sullen unions and floundering around while the big grab goes on to Washington and Moscow." (1957, 124)

The deficiency of American values and the type of world that these values have created are also judged by Sal as they appear personified in the guise of the police. Throughout the novel, Sal and Dean repeatedly encounter cops who harass them, jail them, trail them in the cities, and take their money.[7] In the middle of the book, Paradise finally condemns, in a way that is highly prophetic of the 1960s, this manifestation of the old values: .

> The American police are involved in psychological warfare against those Americans who don't frighten them with imposing papers and threats. It's a Victorian police force; it peers out of musty windows and wants to inquire about everything, and can make crimes if the crimes don't exist to its satisfaction. (1957, 113)

Kerouac later contrasts this image of American police with what he found in Mexico: "Such lovely policemen God hath never wrought in America. No suspicions, no fuss, no bother: he was the guardian of the sleeping town, period" (1957, 242).

What is important in the above discussion is the attitude of social deviance that accentuates the romanticized reality that Kerouac was striving to create; it is the sense of freedom through questioning that Kerouac represents. In the 1950s, most middle-class Americans, whose only negative experience with the police would be traffic violations, would not think of criticizing them. During this time, the police were, as they have usually been, staunch supporters of middle-class privilege and racist ideology (Walker 1980). In contrast, Kerouac's attitude demarcated a demystification of an important American institution, thus contributing to a growing social rift between the police and the white, privileged American public.

Kerouac's perspective polarizes two worldviews and vitalizes an opposition to the psychological and potentially physical oppression of the corporate state. Tytell explains the effect that Kerouac had:

> For many, [On the Road] was the book that most motivated dissatisfaction with the atmosphere of unquestioning acceptance that stifled the fifties; . . . its audience grows and young people gravitate to a force in it that seems to propel by the material itself, almost as if its author did not exist as an outside agency of creation. (1976, 157)

Tytell uses the word "gravitate" to suggest the magnetic quality found in *On the Road*. In an effort to rephrase what Tytell terms as gravitation, I substitute the phrase "chaining-out process." Tytell is merely writing in nonrhetorical terms what Bormann explains as the influence of "dramatizations" in creating spheres of attraction, understanding, and influence:

> The dramatizations which catch on and chain out in small groups are worked into public speeches and into the mass media and, in turn, spread across larger publics, serve to sustain the members' sense of community, to impel them strongly to action . . . and to provide them with a social reality filled with heroes, villains, emotions, and attitudes. (1972, 398)

Dramatizations are, in a sense, self-contained gravitational systems, marked by spheres of influence. People become attracted to dramas and enter orbits around particular visions. In this case, the Vision of Social Deviance is a call to action, a questioning of motivation, and a suggestion for a new social reality with a reordering of priorities. People who read Kerouac's book and enter the orbit of its drama are logologically encouraged to see social deviance as a political and social option. As discussed by Burke, logology is the study of "words about words" (1970, 1). Specifically, logology refers to the relationships *among* words, what words imply for each other in terms of an incipient action (see Bridges 1996). In short, readers who are affected by Kerouac's book learn a vocabulary and an attitude to help them to focus their discontent and to gain the support of others who feel the same way. Readers of the novel are taught that their alienation has roots in a problematic and systemic world and that, in their alienation, they have ideological peers.

6

The Vision of Sexuality

Extending from the general notion of social deviance is the more specific vision of sexuality. For Kerouac, human sexuality is one terrain on which the body becomes political.[1] In expressing social deviance, Kerouac redefines the norms of sexuality in 1950s America, reinventing a significant part of U.S. morality. In mid-century America, much human sexuality was considered a form of social deviance, as it is today (although less so), since sexual activity that falls outside of the traditional bounds of Christian morality is a potential threat to many cultural institutions—explaining in part the fierce resistance to homosexuality in many sectors of American society. Divergent forms of sexuality, particularly homosexuality, undermine many of the foundations upon which "normal" cultural practices are measured. Similarly, Dean Moriarty's sexuality can be evaluated in terms of its implicit threat to the larger social fabric. While ostensibly heterosexual, Dean's flagrant disregard for monogamous relationships—unlike other forms of sexual transgression, such as "machoism"—undermines family norms and values, calling into question some of the basic moralities that structure our society. In no sense can Dean be seen as "macho," although there is a temptation to read him in that way. Dean does not simply have mistresses to emphasize his "manliness"; rather, Dean *consumes* women with such ferocity and mindlessness that other motivations have to be inferred. Dean is more than phallocentric; this "more" is a transcendence that also exceeds base forms of machoism.

Simply, Dean uses sex to transcend the constraints and limitations placed on sexuality by society. These constraints and limitations are not "repressive," however. Rather, they are "productive," as Foucault (1978) suggests: they produce norms governing personal behavior and delineate expectations of responsible and acceptable action. These expectations and responsibilities translate into political realities as well as consciousness potentialities. Any sexual expression is, simultaneously, an expression of a consciousness that has reproductive, religious, and cultural significance (Stein 1992; Vincinus 1982).

The Vision of Sexuality in *On the Road* focuses the general Vision of Social Deviance in specific ways, directing a potential subculture to particular avenues of expression. Any form of social deviance needs to be defined; this definition of what "counts" as deviance finds particular forms of expression depending upon a group's political, social, or cultural objectives. In short, a subculture, like the Beat or hippie subculture, defines social deviance in such a way as to give it political sanction as well as a rhetorical amplification. The sanction for deviance derives from the redescription of a value or norm in a way that has positive connotations for the group (it builds group solidarity) while at the same time it clearly defines the group as oppositional to a value or values within the dominant culture. The sanctioning of deviance also involves amplification, since the rationale for deviance has to be explained and/or justified. By understanding the process of this sanctioning/amplification, a reader can gain a better understanding of what a group *is*. Thus, as Rod Hart acknowledges, fantasy theme analysis "is particularly useful for understanding cultures" (1990, 334).

Sexuality is a central theme in *On the Road*. Both the Vision of Social Deviance and the Vision of Sexuality are representative of a larger archetypal vision and master analogy, the vision of Dean Moriarty as saint and savior, the great redeemer. Dean is presented as a Christlike incarnation of spiritual resurrection and rebirth, and he embodies the holy Kerouac trinity of road, sex, and sainthood. While Dean is clearly a self-destructive character (even Sal constantly remarks how Dean degenerates before his eyes), Kerouac envisions him as leading the assault on the old values, gallantly ushering in the new. Dean embodies the self-sacrifice of the mythic Christ—Dean suffers his madness and other deprivations so that others can learn from his experience. In *On the Road*, Dean appears as an urgent and holy messenger living on the verge of a new and powerful era. Dean inspires others, in particular Sal, to achieve a holiness in their lives. For instance, Sal, in contemplating an early trip East, remarks: "I pictured myself in a Denver bar that night, with all the gang, and in their eyes I would be strange and ragged and like the Prophet who has walked across the land to bring the dark Word, and the only Word I had was 'Wow!'" (1957, 32). The liberating spirituality celebrated in *On the Road* is not easily put into words, as the above quote illustrates. For Kerouac, this spirituality simply is "Wow!" Another way that this spirituality or holiness is expressed is in the pursuit of "IT!" The sense of IT! that Kerouac discusses in conjunction with his expression of "Wow" are indications of a transcendence that takes the reader beyond words (which is ironic considering that Kerouac is working within a prose medium).

Dean clearly inspires Sal and the audience of Kerouac's book to work toward a liberating consciousness. In this sense, Dean is not much different than traditional prophets as found in the Bible. Prophets present countermessages to the values of a society; they warn, they cajole, they persuade by personal examples. Prophets, in short, live out their moralitics and are controversial. Prophets always promise some sort of liberation, usually a sociological liberation based upon a countermorality; this is no less true of Dean, the prophet of Kerouac's vision. An immediate example of Dean's liberating ethos that Sal and readers encounter is the celebration of the libido—the wild sexual drive of the human spirit. After he meets Dean, it becomes immediately obvious to Sal that "sex is the one and only holy and important thing in [Dean's] life" (1957, 6). Sexual energy, raw, pure, and exceedingly abusive to both Dean's body and to all the women Dean and Sal meet, is a primordial force that has been redirected from its construction in puritan culture, grounding most of the motivation and action that appears in *On the Road*. An example of this can be seen as Carlo Marx (modeled after Allen Ginsberg) explains Dean's schedule to Sal:

> "The schedule is this: I came off work a half-hour ago. In that time Dean is balling Marylou at the hotel and gives me time to change and dress. At one he rushes from Marylou to Camille—of course neither one of them knows what's going on—and bangs her once, giving me time to arrive at one-thirty. Then he comes out with me— first he has to beg with Camille, who's already started to hate me— and we come here to talk till six in the morning. We usually spend more time than that, but it's getting awfully complicated and he's pressed for time. Then at six he goes back to Marylou—and he's going to spend all day tomorrow running around to get the necessary papers for their divorce. Marylou's all for it, but she insists on banging in the interim. She says she loves him—so does Camille." (1957, 37)

Clearly, Kerouac is describing a different moral reality than the one experienced by most people in mid-century America. There is a hyperactive consciousness operating underneath this text: a subtext that is first and foremost an attitude toward sex and morality. This subtext is a super-revved-up engine traveling at demonic speeds just underneath our awareness, surfacing at times into consciousness. Nevertheless, the presence of this subtext is always felt; it is a logic, a grammar, and a trajectory of recurring motivations and circumstances.

On one level, Sal's sexual relationships differ from Dean's. For instance, Sal struggles with the faint facade of appearing traditional. Indeed, when compared to Dean's sexual frenzy, Sal appears impotent as a sexual force. But this is just a superficial reading of Sal's sexuality and the influence it has on the sexual politics of the text. Under closer examination, Sal's relationships are as much a clear rejection of conventional values as Dean's. In fact, Dean's sexual antics seem unreal; they are so flagrant, extravagant, and bizarre that it is difficult to see how they are exemplary in and of themselves. Certainly, they establish moral standards, but any myth can do so; it is not so obvious how Dean's sexuality can serve as an example for specific behavior. A more clearly prescriptive sexuality is found in Sal's relationships. With Dean as archetype, the perfect example of sexual exertion, and Sal as the example of a nondescript and colorless "everyman," a careful reader can sense the ideologies and attitudes of sexuality that become more popularly identified as the "sexual revolution" of the 1960s—specifically its more abusive, phallocentric, and misogynist tendencies.[2]

Sal's sexual encounters are metonymic of Dean's flagrant disregard for all but the primacy of his infamous loins. For example, before being exposed to the bulk of his experiences with Dean, Sal engages in a three-week relationship in California with Terry, a young Mexican farm laborer with a small son. During this time, Sal hides from Terry's parents and husband and picks cotton to pay for their meager groceries and tent where they live together as a "family"—a seemingly traditional relationship. At one point, Sal even looks "up at the dark sky and prayed to God for a better break for the little people I loved" (1957, 81).[3] Without taking responsibility for the child, Sal delights in playing with him, while Terry mends Sal's clothes, torn each day by the thorns of the cotton plant—a relatively traditional scene. Unlike Dean who ruthlessly pursues many women at once, Sal is more or less content to lay down "roots," if only for a short time. As Sal explains, "I was a man of the earth, precisely as I had dreamed I would be, in Paterson" (1957, 82).[4]

While the placidity of this domestic experience promises the potential for a more long-term relationship, it is only temporary. Sal's sincerity has its limitations; the experience grows tiresome and Sal declares, "I was through with my chores in the cottonfield. I could feel the pull of my own life calling me back" (1957, 83). While Sal hides in the bushes outside of the small San Joaquin shack of Terry's parents, Terry fights with her family over Sal—she still believes in the sincerity of Sal's traditional persona. However, Terry's discussion with her family is all for naught; Sal has not seriously entertained the idea of taking Terry with him. He sits in the darkness outside, not worried about the trouble he has caused her with her family and husband. Rather, Sal selfishly relishes the moment as if this script is being written for his enjoyment. He exclaims, "I felt like a million dollars; I was adventuring in the crazy American night" (1957, 84).

Sal's sexual "adventure" with a poor woman of color turns out to be her heartbreak.[5] With little explanation, Sal leaves Terry to her *fellahin* fate (a fate romanticized by Kerouac but always from a safe distance), betraying his prayer to God to help those he loved. Sal's only remarks are that "[t]his was the end of something," adding somewhat incomprehensibly that "love is like a duel" (1957, 85). This incident, combined with an earlier sexual scene, severs the last remaining traditional ties that Paradise has with women. From then on, Sal practices Dean's holy message: the experience, not the emotional ties with a woman, is the draw.

An earlier scene better illustrates this point. Sal is fixed up, by Dean, with a woman named Rita Bettencourt, whom Sal describes as being "a nice little girl, simple and true, and tremendously frightened of sex" (1957, 48). We do not learn much else about her: she is faceless, characterless, and without complexity. This woman is simply an object, a thing to have sex with. Her worth, her usefulness, is severely compromised by her sexual timidity, and Sal quickly moves to correct this. He tells her that sex is beautiful and convinces her to let him prove it. But what does he say? More importantly, what precedent exists in Sal's world that would lead him to be able to argue his proposition honestly? We know that Sal was married and that the marriage was terrible, but nothing more. Dean is introduced in the opening pages as having sex with everyone he can: in the back of cars, everywhere. He is always naked when in his apartment and speaks to women in vulgar ways. The "beauty" of sex is never evident in *On the Road*. Indeed, Sal's impatience gets the better of him after he talks the "little," "simple," and "true" girl into bed and fails to prove anything. "She sighed in the dark" (1957, 48), and Sal appears to feel some degree of shame for his actions.

This shame, however, is without moral direction, at least in a traditional sense. Sal is moved to assuage his guilt, and he does this by shifting blame from himself to her. This is a subtle transference, one that makes her responsible for their lifeless sex. He asks her, "What do you want out of life?" (1957, 48). In response, Rita yawns, a classic Kerouac faux pas. She evidently is committed to the values that Sal is rejecting: she wants to get along by waiting on tables. The transfer of blame is now complete—there is something wrong with the woman for being so uninspired. There is also remorse. Yet again, it is an unreflexive remorse directed at God rather than at Sal's own actions:

> I put my hand over her mouth and told her not to yawn. I tried to tell her how excited I was about life and the things we could do together; saying that and planning to leave Denver in two days. She turned

away wearily. We lay on our backs, looking at the ceiling and wondering what God had wrought when He made life so sad. (1957, 48)

As the facade of the traditional romance dissipates, Sal becomes altogether envious of Dean's sexual prowess: Dean's sexuality becomes the norm of sexual activity that is aspired to in the book. Sexually speaking, what begins with Sal's messy divorce and his feeble attempts to have traditional relationships ends in the brothels of Mexico at the novel's conclusion. Sal describes one scene:

> I was set upon by a fat and uninteresting girl with a puppy dog, who got sore at me when I took a dislike to the dog because it kept trying to bite me. She compromised by putting it away in the back, but by the time she returned I had been hooked by another girl, better looking but not the best, who clung to my neck like a leech. I was trying to break loose to get at a sixteen-year-old colored girl who sat gloomily inspecting her navel through an opening in her short shirty dress across the hall. I couldn't do it. Stan had a fifteen-year-old girl with an almond-colored skin and a dress that was buttoned half-way down and halfway up. It was mad. A good twenty men leaned in that window, watching. (1957, 236)

Sex becomes a perverse spectacle of colonization and consumption. The women are not even whores: they are leeches. More critically, they are children; Sal has the gall to berate a little girl for her dog, forcing her to "compromise" before having sex with him. For Sal this is a "mad" scene ("mad" being Kerouac's favorite, most positive adjective). Sal is disappointed because he is denied a sixteen-year-old. He ends up sleeping with the "leech" and pays her three and a half dollars (1957, 236).

While Sal admits to feeling ashamed at times and makes excuses for his behavior, Dean makes no pretense about sexual relationships existing for any other reason than his own insatiable ends. To the women he uses and abuses, Dean returns little more than the satisfaction of his near-legendary sexual exertions. Dean traverses both this country and Mexico in a mad tirade of adultery, bigamy, wife-sharing, divorce, marriage, pregnancies, and innumerable one-night stands, even though he "had to sweat and curse to make a living" (1957, 6), remarks Sal, obviously impressed. This sexual theme permeates the novel, challenging traditional mores. In place of traditional perspectives on sexuality, Kerouac, through his description of Dean Moriarty, offers "an ideal . . . of release and joy experienced by the less materially privileged segments of the society" (Tytell 1976, 159).

To a large extent, Kerouac's perspective is an act of extreme social and moral irresponsibility, free license and fallacious justification for the acquaintance rape and sexual abuse that has been committed in the name of "sexual freedom." As the above passages suggest, Kerouac is promoting a male privilege of sexual conquest—the more exotic the women, the more marginalized and impoverished, the better the sex. In a scene from *The Subterraneans*, Kerouac writes longingly of Mardou, a half black, one-quarter Cherokee woman:

> So I went home and for several days in sexual phantasies was she, her dark feet, thongs of sandals, dark eyes, little soft brown face, Rita-Savage-like cheeks and lips, little secretive intimacy and somehow now softly snakelike charm as befits a little thin brown woman disposed to wearing dark clothes, poor, beat subterranean clothes. (1958c, 11)

The "Rita Savage" evoked is an older white girl, a friend of Kerouac's sister. Kerouac refers to Rita longingly, but she had denied him. Prevented access to her body, Kerouac explains how he fantasizes fellatio with Rita—vulgarly describing her kneeling in front of him while he sits on the toilet.

Notice the fictional name, "Savage," that Kerouac gives to this woman who provokes his sexual appetites. Rita is a white woman who refuses to do the "nasty," savage, erotic things from which white girls stereotypically recoil. Upon seeing Mardou, he is immediately reminded of his fantasies of fellatio and transfers this repressed lust from the unattainable white woman to the attainable woman of color whom he seduces. Mardou becomes a primordial sexual object for Kerouac, one that he *can* attain. Through Mardou, Kerouac enacts his sexual fantasies that were inspired by Rita Savage. The identification of Mardou with "savage" sexuality is so complete that Kerouac attributes to her a "love" for "sadistic treatment" (1958c, 9).

Ironically, while clearly misogynist and destructive, Kerouac's sexual perspective represents an important artistic and social force that helped shock this nation into recognition that it had long denied a powerful human desire that demanded attention. Even though the Vision of Sexuality is abusive, sexist, and degenerative, it also represents a process of social awareness, a new thinking about sexuality. Kerouac's vision leads to more than merely a specific outcome, such as individual sexual activity or abuse. Gregory Stephenson reveals that while Dean "is a prophet of the libido, of the instincts and appetites . . . his desperate hedonism is not, however, an end in itself but rather a means to an end: the transcendence of personal consciousness and time" (1990, 155). Sexual activity is a means to a transcendent goal, the pursuit of IT! Thus, with knowledge of the Vision of Sexuality, it is not paradoxical that the characters of *On the Road* can be self-serving in terms of their pelvic exertions while lamenting, at the same time, the negative implications of human sexuality, as Sal does:

> Boys and girls in America have such a sad time together; sophistication demands that they submit to sex immediately without proper preliminary talk. Not courting talk—real straight talk about souls, for life is holy and every moment is precious. (1957, 49)

Both the Vision of Sexuality and the Vision of Social Deviance from which it extends are localized in Dean Moriarty. Yet Dean is more than merely a character in a novel. As suggested above, he is the archetype of social deviance and of sexuality. Dean, himself, is a vision that is deeply ingrained in the transcendent-spiritual tradition of Judeo-Christian culture.

7

Dean as Vision

Neal Cassady was a troubled and deeply disturbed human being who would not outlive the 1960s. However, the vision that he inspired in others, particularly in Jack Kerouac and Ken Kesey, would. Their visions of Cassady encouraged large collective identities of individuals who gathered and shared common dreams of self-(re)creation. In other words, Dean as Vision helps establish a general ideological discourse. Such ideological discourse is important to understand from a communication perspective because, as Maurice Charland explains, the "collective identities forming the base of rhetorical appeals themselves depend upon rhetoric. . . . [Social phenomena,] in general, exist only through an ideological discourse that constitutes them" (1987, 139).

As argued in part 1 of this study, *On the Road* is an ideological statement that was a significant force in the creation of a nationwide collective identity. Dennis Sean McNally writes that in 1967 the "tribes of flower-bedecked American pilgrims [that] came together in San Francisco's Golden Gate Park . . . were the direct heirs of *On the Road*." In addition, McNally notes that Jerry Garcia, Janis Joplin, and many other influential figures and emblems of the 1960s "acknowledged their roots to a prior Beat Generation" (1979, 325). For example, as Ray Manzarek testifies, "If Jack Kerouac had never written *On the Road*, The Doors would never have existed" (qtd. in Rhino 1990, 20). For this group of people, Dean as Vision best exemplifies the rhetorical appeals of Kerouac's ideology. As Charland elaborates, "Ideology is material existing not in the realm of ideas, but in that of material practices. Ideology is material because subjects enact their ideology and reconstitute their material world in its image" (1987, 143).

One catalyst for this enactment is Dean as Vision. As Kerouac's vision, Dean becomes the material substance of a vague ideological commitment. All ideological commitments are vague, at least initially, and assume greater specificity and rigidity after years of group participation. Ideologies assume their material presence in the world through interpretation and action; ideology is nothing if it is not the practice or manifestation of a value commitment. Ideologies expand only as people accept the values of that ideology and manifest them in some kind of material commitment (that is, behavior, attitude, or value). With this in mind, this chapter illustrates how Kerouac ideologized an American landscape and many of its people with the development of Dean as Vision.

The subject matter of *On the Road* is America, particularly its soul. This soul is not a religious soul but a romantic soul, the transcendent spirituality that Dean comes to exemplify. In searching for the soul of America, Kerouac's writing is constantly torn between a romanticism for the past, inspired by Wolfe and Goethe, and an anticipation of a future being built, largely by young adventure-seeking people like Kerouac and modeled after Dean. Kerouac believes that the past is important, and throughout his writing, he looks back toward an earlier, simpler time of "true" innocence, an alternative consciousness. Kerouac approaches the future from the past. The past that Kerouac imagines is untamed, its people unrestrained. In the present that Kerouac rejects, restraints have been enacted. People have been caged; emotions have been chained. In Dean, Kerouac presents the harbinger of future American values. People like Dean had been hidden away, but no more. These people, according to Sal, "were like the man with the dungeon stone and the gloom, rising from the underground, the sordid hipsters of America, a new beat generation that I was slowly joining" (1957, 46).

But what had happened to open the floodgates? Why were these people coming up from the dungeon? What inspired Kerouac's vision and why was it alluring? Tytell explains how Kerouac and his "Beat Generation" were responding to some fundamental incongruities taking place in America:

> [B]ecause of the depression and the anticipation of the [Second World] [W]ar . . . a great fissure had occurred in the American psyche, an uprooting of family relationships, of the sense of place and community that was compounded by a fear of imminent devastation. It was a shared premonition that the entire society was going to be changed in a major way, and that young men were to be particularly sacrificed. (1976, 9)

In the late 1940s and early 1950s the old consciousness, the corporate fantasy of capitalism, had glossed over the importance of this fissure and instead focused American consciousness on the tremendous prosperity that the country was experiencing. The promises of the future were too glorious to allow Americans to ponder the implications of this fissure for men and women coming to grips with the increasing weight of the twentieth century. As a result, the culture that Kerouac was responding to was a house of cards. The abyss was near. The culture of Kerouac's era teetered on the brink of moral collapse (as evidenced by the American war on Korea and, later, on Vietnam). The contradictions and ironies that led to a widespread fear of "imminent devastation" still exist and the tensions they cause are just as real; consequently, the time remains ripe for a new set of cultural identifications.

Political identifications are significant, accentuating the role that rhetoric plays in cultural politics. As the theoretical apparatus of this book suggests, a rhetorical vision popularizes a fantasy with an audience and congregates individuals to create a new community. This is another way of saying that fantasy involves the rhetoric of identification. As Bormann explains, rhetorical visions work when "people create a common consciousness by becoming aware that they are involved in an identifiable group and that their group differs in some important respects from other groups" (1985, 11). As such, group members acknowledge their uniqueness—via the shared fantasy—through the means of a specific identification device. This rhetorical device serves a function of creating a cultural context for consubstantiality to occur within a localized group. As discussed by Kenneth Burke, person X is consubstantial to Y (sharing perceived substance) when X becomes identified with Y. X and Y are intrinsically different entities with separate cognitive and neurological systems and are only identified with each other by an overt act of definition, association, or will by either X or Y. This is the primary function of rhetoric, according to Burke, to build or to separate consubstantial relationships (1969b). Burke explains one level on which consubstantiality operates with the example of the politician "who, though rich, tells humble constituents of his humble origins" (1972, 28; see Gibson 1970).

Identification devices come in many different forms. A human individual, a species of animal, a natural force, or an idea can all serve as anchors to ground metaphors for group coherence. When they do so, they become animated with social significance and are placed within the governing cultural grammar. For example, Ronald Reagan, the Democratic donkey, a football team called the Tornadoes, and the New Deal are examples of metaphor-producing anchors that aid in the consubstantial act, enabling aligned group members to emulate or personify the phenomenon. As a man, Ronald Reagan is uninspiring and no different from all other Homo sapiens who, in and of themselves, have no special meaning. Yet as a symbol, he stands for a particular type of political unity. The name conjures up differing connotations. While the name "Ronald Reagan" is not exactly a metaphor, it is metonymic. As discussed by Burke, metonymy is a reduction, a representation, one of the four master tropes by which people come to understand their worlds (1969a, 503–17). Burke explains that the function of metonymy is "to convey some incorporeal or intangible state in terms of the corporeal or tangible" (1969a, 506); in a general sense, this is also the function of metaphor. My other three examples are clearly metaphors; they are devices "for seeing something *in terms of* something else." Metaphors bring out "the thisness of a that, or the thatness of a this" (Burke 1969a, 503).[1]

Kerouac's vision, then, is both metonymic and metaphoric. His vision is transcendent and thus something that cannot easily be expressed in words. It needs to be reduced and embodied and represented by what people commonly know. Thus, Kerouac grounds his vision in Cassady who, as Dean Moriarty, becomes a symbol of a new value system. Subsequently, Beat culture personified itself in Kerouac, as if *he* were the ideals that his character Dean Moriarty represents. These visions of Kerouac served the function of what Bormann calls "innovation dramas" (1985, 11). Innovation dramas represent those discourses in which a consciousness is created and disseminated through a population by an initially small message that is picked up and elaborated upon by members of a group. These dramas represent adaptive or significant changes in a prior vision, thus encouraging group unity or common consubstantiality among members of the new culture. Bormann elaborates on how innovation dramas work to promote and develop a collective fantasy theme:

> People caught up in a chain of fantasies . . . feed back ideas and new dramatizations to add to the original comment; messages begin flowing rapidly among the participants until, under the suggestive power of the group fantasy, the constraints that normally hold people back are released; they feel free to experiment with ideas, to play with concepts, wild suggestions, and imaginative notions. Soon a number of people are deeply involved with the discussion, excitedly adding their emotional support and often modifying the ongoing script. (1985, 11)

Similar to Bormann's explanation, Kerouac's dramas, as exemplified in Dean Moriarty, constitute a significant departure from the previous visions and fantasies of society. Gerald Nicosia notes that, in effect, Kerouac "was telling people that they didn't need cars and refrigerators to be happy" (1984, 2). This position clashed with the consumer-based fantasy that encompassed much of American culture at the time, as well as today. Kerouac challenged the dominant myth of American culture and wrote to replace it with his own. Vast numbers of people felt similarly, as evidenced by the power of the counterculture at the end of the 1960s.

In McGee's study of ideologically constitutive discourse, this sort of phenomenon is presented in the following fashion:

> [A new] rhetoric emerges when masses of people begin to *respond* to a myth, not only by exhibiting collective behavior, but also by publicly ratifying the transition wherein they give up control over their individual destinies for the sake of a dream. (1975, 243)

In *On the Road*, the Vision of Dean accomplishes what Bormann suggests when he writes, "One way for groups of people to develop radically new rhetorical visions is to take a contemporary vision and stand it on its head" (1985, 11).

Disrupting an old vision often involves celebrating the values and images repressed by the established order, as when anti-Vietnam War protesters flew the North Vietnamese flag at their rallies. In Kerouac's world, this act of resistance occurs when Sal's values encompass the freedom associated with childhood exuberance, with the trials of the *fellahin*, with the human perseverance and woeful joys of the African American, then referred to as "Negroes." Dean had already achieved the state described by Kerouac below, but it is a state toward which Sal constantly strives:

> [W]ishing I were a Negro feeling that the best that the white world had offered was not enough ecstasy for me, not enough life, joy, kicks, darkness, not enough night. . . . I wished I were a Denver Mexican, or even a poor overworked Jap, anything but what I was so drearily, a "white man" disillusioned. All my life I'd had white ambitions. (1957, 148)

This theme, challenging our emotive feelings for common, everyday expectations, is an important rhetorical tactic in the novel. While Kerouac is condescending, he nevertheless symbolically slaps the face of traditional America. Kerouac is not disrespectful to African Americans, although the passage above and the one discussed below can certainly be interpreted in that way. Rather, in the white world of racist America, a racism more real and dangerous than Kerouac's romantic naïveté, expressing solidarity with black people and, worse, desiring to become the "Other" is often met with grave consequences (cf. Bhabba 1994, Said 1978). Kerouac's challenge to white culture is more evident in the next passage:

> A gang of colored women came by, and one of the young ones detached herself from motherlike elders and came to me fast —"Hello Joe!"—and suddenly saw it wasn't, and ran back, blushing. I wished I were Joe. I was only myself, Sal Paradise, sad, strolling in this vio-

lent dark, this unbearably sweet night, wishing I could exchange worlds with the happy, true-hearted, ecstatic Negroes of America. (1957, 149)

This passage is obviously problematic in its representation of the African American, whom Kerouac portrays paternalistically, as he does *all* minorities; yet, he never does so maliciously, and this is the most extreme example of it in *On the Road*. His condescending tone must be discounted in light of Kerouac's larger poetic framework. Kerouac typically poeticized the world, and this is particularly evident in his books of reminiscence and of his childhood, novels such as *Maggie Cassady* (1959a), *Dr. Sax* (1958a), and *Visions of Gerard* (1963).[2]

Kerouac's intent as a writer is to poeticize life and thus circumvent its many sufferings and woe; he refers to himself as a "jazz poet" who works in a prose medium. Such intent is not always obvious, and this misreading of Kerouac helped fuel the establishment's condemnation of him. In particular, Podhoretz caustically condemns Kerouac for, among other things, his portrayal of African Americans in the above two quotes:

> It will be news to the Negroes to learn that they are so happy and ecstatic; I doubt if a more idyllic picture of Negro life has been painted since certain Southern ideologies tried to convince the world that things were fine as fine could be for the slaves on the old plantation. (1958, 311)

Like many critics of Kerouac, Podhoretz has engaged in the willful misinterpretation of context. As mentioned above, Kerouac is not a racist but a romantic, and while he alters our perceptions of reality with his prose, he provokes a rhetorical vision that is ultimately rooted in resistance and redescription. Kerouac's vision is connected with the African American experience at the time that Kerouac wrote—a time that did not encourage a clearheaded and honest appraisal of the institution of cultural and economic apartheid.

A scene from *The Subterraneans*, a book describing Kerouac's relationship with an African American woman, exemplifies my point that Kerouac uses African American culture as inspiration for his vision and as an act of resistance to a Eurocentric corporate consciousness. In this scene, Kerouac expresses solidarity with Mardou's father, half Cherokee, "because I'd been out there and sat on the ground and seen the . . . steel of America covering the ground filled with the bones of old Indians and Original Americans" (1958c, 20). In a sense, Kerouac is a witness to a site of domination that had, in the late 1950s, yet to gain a critical visibility.

A similar point can be made of Mardou's "blackness" as with her father's "redness." Kerouac finds in her "blackness" a moving, powerful story of the spiritual strength that first drove him to search on the road:

> [N]o girl had ever moved me with a story of spiritual suffering and so beautifully her soul showing out radiant as an angel wandering in hell and the selfsame streets I'd roamed in watching, watching for someone just like her and never dreaming the darkness and the mystery . . . (1958c, 36)

As the above illustrates, Kerouac rejects the Eurocentric aspects of U.S. culture that prevents white people from empathizing with "blackness" but does so in a way that intentionally misrepresents African American culture (as well as other marginalized ethnic groups) (see Panish 1994). Kerouac celebrates what he believes are the virtues of "blackness," and he sees those virtues in Dean, who is, in many symbolic ways, "black" himself, or at least a cultural "Other."

In particular, Kerouac believes that the African American experience, while involving a repressed culture, affords its people opportunities denied to Sal in the pursuit of IT! (cf. Mailer 1958). The juxtaposition of the Euro-American and the African American worlds in *On the Road* is a part of Dean as Vision because, of all Kerouac's characters, Dean comes closest to identifying with the experiences of the African American world. This point involves the liminal experience: African Americans were in the 1940s and 1950s, as many continue to be today, marginalized from the American middle-class experience (Berry and Blassingame 1982). The black experience in the United States has always been a marginalized one, thus giving many African Americans a forced liminality. In their own quest for liminality, as discussed in chapter 8, Sal and Dean feel a particular affinity and admiration for the African American experience. Granted, they were not working toward the eradication of racism; rather, both men were "poaching" (de Certeau 1984), borrowing the language, music, drugs, and despair of a repressed people in order to redescribe their own positions. Kerouac uses the marginal experience of the African American to learn something about his own self-description.

With disdain, bell hooks discusses this phenomenon of white poaching of the black cultural experience. In particular, she discusses Madonna, but her critique is equally applicable to other poachers:

> White women "stars" like Madonna, Sandra Bernhard, and many others publicly name their interest in, and appropriation of, black culture as yet another sign of their radical chic. Intimacy with that "nasty" blackness good white girls stay away from is what they seek.

To white and other non-black consumers, this gives them a special
flavor, an added spice. After all it is a very recent historical phenomenon for any white girl to be able to get some mileage out of flaunt-
ing her fascination and envy with blackness. The thing about envy
is that it is always ready to destroy, erase, take-over, and consume
the desired object. That's exactly what Madonna attempts to do
when she appropriates and commodifies aspects of black culture.
(1992, 157)

There is some degree to which hooks's critique of Madonna can be
applied to Kerouac—but only some. Kerouac honestly feels as if his
"white" existence is limiting of a wider, more "real" existence, and he is
correct to a certain degree: in addition to its advantages, social privilege
has its social limitations, particularly in terms of sexual mores. Both
Kerouac and Madonna are trying to expand these limitations, albeit for
different motivations and with different levels of integrity.

While Sal Paradise experiences the thoughts and feelings of cultural
alienation from the middle-class white world, Dean embodies them.
Literally, Dean is, body and soul, the antithesis of "white man's am-
bition." Dean is the "Other," the white man who refuses to uphold the
expectations of his "race" and class and who, instead, chooses to
redefine those expectations, challenging others to do so as well. He
represents the breakdown of the "white man's morality," accentuating
its hypocrisy and the false sense of self-importance that it cultivates. As
Stephenson notes, "Dean is protean, as powerful, and as unknowable
as the human subconscious mind with which he may be identified—as
a votary, a prophet, and as an embodiment of its energies and
mysteries" (1990, 158). Dean, the son of a wino, was raised begging on
the streets of Denver's skid row, was jailed repeatedly for stealing cars,
and exhibits all the stereotypical sexual behaviors attributed to the
black man. Essentially, Dean lives a black man's life as a poor, disenfranchised member of the American underclass.

Like most African Americans in the 1950s, Dean never had the car-
rot of prosperity dangled before him, the promise of wealth and status
that provokes the conformity rewarding America's white privileged class.
Dean is uncorrupted by the old consciousness; he is similar to a child who
is raised in the woods by wolves and who returns to civilization without
the limiting notions that society forces upon its citizens. Sal senses this
purity in Dean's mad conversations, which are incomprehensible to all,
including Dean. Dean speaks from somewhere "else," and his words and
deeds have the power to transport people to that other world. Dean's
apparent confusion is acceptable to Sal and to readers of Kerouac's book,
because the rationality of discourse that Dean rejects, or never learned,
represents limitations of thought and consciousness, a prescriptive way

of being that is found in what Sal refers to as "paper America" (1957, 90). Accentuating this point is the fact that Neal Cassady himself wrote very little (1971, 1977, 1993). He was beyond words, beyond the limitations of the page; Dean exemplifies the immediacy of the spoken word, the experience that gives language its life and significance. At times of complete understanding or intense experiences when Sal and Dean simply cannot express themselves through language, they are able to "understand each other on other levels of madness" (1957, 7). Stephenson explains that through mediums of communication other than language, "Dean advises a total acceptance of oneself and of the world without resistance or despair, an attention and a response to circumstances that amount to a cosmic optimism" (1990, 157).

When he realizes that Dean is able to transcend the weariness of life and that Dean serves as a catalyst for Sal's own redescriptions, Sal is transformed and is separated from the death and illness encountered at the beginning of the novel. In Dean, Sal sees "a kind of holy lightning . . . flashing from his excitement and his vision" (1957, 8). Little is the same for Sal or for significant social aspects of American culture after the first few pages of *On the Road*, as Kerouac begins his "courageous response to the dominating passivity of his time" (Tytell 1976, 12). Inspired by his new sense of lateral deviance or agitation, Kerouac exclaims, "The whole mad swirl of everything to come began . . . it would mix up my friends and all I have left of my family in a big dust cloud over the American night" (1957, 8).

In Sal's testimony we find Dean's brilliance as the "holy goof" (1957, 160): the burning antidote to everything that is ill in civilization; the madman convict who infuses life into both Kerouac and, by Kerouac's influence, a larger body in American culture; the single embodiment of a new vision for America, a vision earned "from the Natural Tailor of Natural Joy" (1957, 10); the man "who had the tremendous energy of a new kind of American saint" (34); "a Western Kinsman of the sun" (11); "a wild yea-saying of American joy" (11); "something new, long prophesied, long a-coming" (11). Stephenson points out that for Sal, and for Kerouac's audience who internalized Kerouac's rhetorical vision, "the Cassady figure represents something archetypally American, something closely connected with American literature, American history, and with deep-seated patterns of the American psyche" (1990, 159). According to Gary Snyder, Kerouac's portrayal of Cassady has a special appeal that lies deep in the American psyche:

> Cassady was like so many Americans who had inherited that taste for the limitless, for no limits, which was a unique American experience. You can get hooked on that if you don't know how to trans-

late it into other regions, since when the sheer physical space dissipates you go crazy. (qtd. in Charters 1973, 287)

This is Dean, the man who has "got the secret that we're all busting to find and it's splitting his head wide open" (1957, 161). Dean Moriarty, modern day Christopher Smart, was "by virtue of his enormous sins . . . becoming the Idiot, the Imbecile, the Saint of the lot" (1957, 160). Upon reaching this state of existence, Sal notices that Dean "was BEAT—the root, the soul of Beatific" (1957, 161). With the religious fervor of his saintliness, Dean exemplifies the freedom that most people fail to achieve. As Stephenson explains, "Cassady's role as catalyst . . . extended to that of a cultural catalyst, his energies inspiring and helping to define the shape and direction of postwar American culture" (1990, 164). Stephenson elaborates on the importance of Kerouac's description of Neal Cassady:

> What the Cassady figure represents in American literature and culture is a populist mysticism: the reemergence of a heterodox, syncretic, religious impulse that has previously found expression in such figures as Whitman and Henry Miller. The Cassady figure is an embodiment of transcendental primitivism—the American response to the cultural-spiritual crisis of Western civilization to which such movements as dadaism, surrealism, and existentialism have been the European response. (1990, 170)

The promise of Dean's potential is immensely sexual, spiritual, and transcendent: "I knew there'd be girls, visions, everything; somewhere along the line the Pearl would be handed to me" (1957, 11). Here we find the antithetical positioning between the two visions: the one Sal is rejecting, the "American Dream," the corporate psychosis, the work ethic, the belief in uninhibited progress, and the one Kerouac is promoting through Dean, the simple wisdom earned from the dust and air of the great "raw land" (1957, 253).

Dean as Vision represents a unifying fantasy theme grounding both the Vision of Social Deviance and the Vision of Sexuality. Dean as Vision, furthermore, is a natural extension of Kerouac's deep religious sentiment that runs throughout *On the Road* (Schwartz 1976). This religious flavor has a peculiar Kerouacian twist, as if Kerouac is trying to Easternize Christianity and produce a hybrid, what I have called in this study the "cult of high experience." Dean, the embodiment of this culture, "was tremendously excited about everything he saw, everything he talked about, every detail of every moment that passed. He was out of his mind with real belief" (1957, 99). This excitement had transformational qualities: "People were now beginning to look at Dean with maternal and paternal affection glowing in their eyes. He was finally an Angel as I always knew he would become" (1957, 215). Holmes describes, in other terms, the role of Dean as Vision in Kerouac's rhetorical fantasy:

> What differentiated the characters in *On the Road* from the slum-bred petty criminals and icon-smashing Bohemians which have been something of a staple in much modern American fiction—what made them beat—was something which seemed to irritate critics most of all. It was Kerouac's insistence that actually they were on a quest, and that the specific object of their quest was spiritual. Though they rushed back and forth across the country on the slightest pretext, gathering kicks along the way, their real journey was inward; and if they seemed to trespass most boundaries, legal and moral, it was only in the hope of finding a belief on the other side. "The Beat Generation," [Kerouac] said, "is basically a religious generation." (1967, 117)

The Beat experience was first and foremost a spiritual quest, a quest for meaning and a search for the "more" (James 1985). In other words, Beat culture was a culture of transcendence that spoke for a wisdom and politics that exceeded the Cold War mentality that had paralyzed the moral, spiritual, and cultural development of the United States.

Kerouac's three visions suggest an intentional rhetoric, an attempt to promote an alternative consciousness. These visions inform the reader that Kerouac—far from being inartistic, a "typist" as he was unaffectionately labeled by Truman Capote (qtd. in Nicosia 1994, 588)—is an artist who uses art not as an aesthetic experience but as an instrument for social change. The three visions discussed help substantiate my claim that Kerouac, through *On the Road*, provides American culture with an alternative to the post-World War II American consciousness. Charland reminds us that such rhetorical visions are steeped with an epistemic significance: "In the telling of a story of a [culture], a [culture] comes to be. It is within the formal structures of a narrative history that it is possible to conceive of a set of individuals as if they were but one" (1987, 140).

Furthermore, we have also seen how fantasy theme analysis enables the reader to locate the parameters of a rhetorical community and to understand the process of intricate symbol exchange among participants of that drama. In the case of *On the Road*, the parameters of the rhetorical community comprise the sub- and countercultures of the 1950s and 1960s. Individuals may have a rhetorical relationship with the book if the fantasy themes contained within the text have a chaining-out effect on them.

Through an understanding of the drama in the text, I suggest that much of the agitation, sexuality, and messianic fervor in *On the Road* contribute to a larger group's fantasy-derived norms. Bormann goes as far as to argue that "[m]uch of what has commonly been thought of as persuasion can be accounted for on the basis of group and mass fantasies" (1985, 9). The fantasizing, in this case the promotion of three visions, is marked by considerable emotional arousal. Bormann explains how this aroused state, implicit in the thematic nature of chained fantasies, functions to serve the individual in his or her struggle to incorporate new experience into meaningful patterns:

> The unfolding experience is often chaotic and confusing. Fantasy themes, in contrast with experience, are organized and artistic. When people dramatize an event, they must select certain characters to be the focus of the story and present them in a favorable light while selecting others to be portrayed in a more negative fashion. (1985, 9)

The Vision of Social Deviance, the Vision of Sexuality, and Dean as Vision serve their hosts by turning personal experience into meaningful constructs. Each vision assumes a unique way of structuring one's individual relationship with other people. The visions work through an implicit morality that finds value in emotional arousal. The aroused state stimulates interest in an individual's immediate social reality and helps dictate the parameters of behavior among members of a community. In exploring these fantasy themes, the reader is able to understand better the rhetorical dimensions of *On the Road* that help make the novel an enduring and socially significant artifact.

8

Conclusion: Kerouac and Liminality

The three visions of *On the Road* involve restless assertions of movement, as if stasis itself is a sign of mortality. Kerouac himself embraces the physical and spiritual notions of travel; the mention of his name conjures the image of both these constructs. Even the title of his novel suggests this quality. Indeed, the title offers a key to unlock what is, for this study, the "final" implications of the text, what I argue is the impetus behind Kerouac's fantasy themes and rhetorical vision.

In arriving at our final destination, it is especially important to remind readers that this stop is just a layover. As both Kerouac and Richard Rorty suggest in their respective writings, the important "meanings" in life, the lessons we learn through the exposure to different people and different lifestyles, are the travels, not the arrivals, the texts—in their ability to instill in us compassion and solidarity—not the interpretations. According to Rorty, it is the *experience* of a text that changes us, moves us to redefine our own private relationships with self and others. It is our involvement with texts, not the professionalized interpretations by theorists, that advances the cause of a more just and compassionate world. He specifically argues, "[W]hen you weigh the good and the bad the social novelists have done against the good and the bad the social theorists have done, you find yourself wishing that there had been more novels and fewer theories" (1991, 80). Nevertheless, critical readings are *didactic*—they move audiences toward particular readings and intellectual commitments that might otherwise be easily overlooked. Rorty provides precedence for such readings when he discusses Vladimir Nabokov and George Orwell. He argues that "[b]oth of them warn the liberal ironist intellectual against temptations to be cruel. Both of them dramatize the tensions between private irony and liberal hope" (1989, 144). Rorty arrives at such conclusions by reading the works of both authors against the backdrop of his neopragmatism.[1]

Academic readings by professional critics are important supplements—not substitutes—for private readings, because they remind us that our personal experiences of a text are often closed experiences. In an important sense, they open up new vistas from which we can contemplate our next life-move. Critics remind us that, while we inevitably end at conclusions, as journeys end at arrivals, these resting points (for that is what they are) must be seen as temporary; they are places to catch our breath before we move on to other places.

Specifically, *On the Road* is a novel that describes a transitory universe of perpetual travel and reluctant arrivals, a world void of stability. Kerouac experiences a hectic blur of life in the fast lane, a landscape and a mindscape seen from a terminal velocity. In Kerouac's narrative, Sal and Dean pass through each other's lives and pass by the world at large with hardly more than a thought. In effect, Sal and Dean are functionally rootless, floating through life on impulse.

In the case of Sal, we find a man who belongs to a middle-class existence but who chooses to sever his ties. But while Sal steps out of his middle-class lifestyle, he fails to step into another sphere of substance. Although Sal partakes of Dean's world, he does not join it, nor does he join the world of the *fellahin*. Consequently, Sal becomes, even more so than Dean, a liminal figure—Dean is, after all, largely incomprehensible, more firmly entrenched in the "other" world than is Sal. The visions Sal offers through the narration of *On the Road* arise from the insights gained by liminality, the position between two worlds. The metaphor of traveling "on the road" is the perfect expression of Sal's liminal state. The strength of the novel, the breadth of its appeals, and the raw material for the creation of three fantasy themes derive from the characteristic qualities of liminality.

Liminality is the term social scientists frequently use to describe the rites of passage that adolescents undergo in tribal communities. As observed by anthropologists, in particular Victor Turner, young people in tribal societies frequently pass through a topology of stages in order to become full-fledged members of their communities; these stages are the "preliminary," the "liminal," and the "post-liminal" (Turner 1969). In the liminal stage, these young people ritualistically transcend their pubescent consciousness, as well as the community consciousness that they will later assume—they "go" somewhere else. That "other" place is a place that breaks from the cultural dialectic and enables the child-person to assume a more structured role as an adult in society. In these cultures, liminality is a process of self-marginalization through which a more thorough cultural integration takes place. The concept provides researchers with an important way to access the central role of symbols in the construction of human social reality. An appreciation of the liminal experience adds to our understanding of Kerouac as a cultural rhetorician.[2]

In discussing Hispanic literature, Gustavo Perez Firmat describes the liminal process as a threefold integration of ritual that leads from separation to marginality and back to reaggregation. Liminality, for him and other scholars, "is a phase, a fleeting, ephemeral moment designed for supersession" (1986, xiii). In literature, liminality functions at the point between two stages in the development of a character. Sal, for instance, belongs neither to the old, outgrown, or rejected reality, nor to the new consciousness that he is striving to define. Sal is in a liminal state. In the condition of liminality, Sal gains a unique perspective on both worlds. His is the visionary's experience from which a new view of social reality is formed. However, such a position cannot long be maintained, nor, by definition, can it last; hence Sal's refrain "Everything was collapsing" expressed at the points in the novel in which his liminal position is threatened by the encroachment of a recalcitrant or dominant reality. Visions, themselves, become dominant realities or else are refuted, leaving the visionary encapsulated again in the structure of the old confinement. Another result is for the visionary to wither and die with the fading remnants of past experience. Either way, the liminal position is a precarious one.

Firmat reminds readers of the danger implicit in the state of liminality when the experience itself is "looked upon not only as a transition between states but as a state in itself, for there exist individuals, groups, or social categories for which the liminal 'movement' turns into a permanent condition" (1986, xiv). Jeanne Murry Walker elaborates on this predicament:

> It is dangerous for the individual to be bereft of a social position and equally dangerous for the society to be challenged by the lack of the initiate's definition. Since the initiate is passing through cultural territory which is unknown, he has ambiguous characteristics; he lacks any clear prescriptive for relationships to others. It is possible for him to become trapped in this unknown territory outside the social structure with no identity, a position which is tantamount to social death. (1987, 115)

It is relevant here to mention that both Jack Kerouac and Neal Cassady, the flesh-and-blood prototypes of Sal and Dean, died tragically as burned-out shells after many years of suffering; their deaths were a mockery of their younger promise and potential. As these men passed from their liminal positions to the demands of the world, they were unable to adjust;

they tried to recapture their experiences through the use of drugs and alcohol, or else they remained fixated in their liminal states and were denied the substance that comes from steady work, family, or respectability. In either case, Kerouac and Cassady represent the ritualistic self-abuse that marred the consciousness of the 1960s counterculture and led to many casualties.[3] However, due to their insubstantial existence as members in the moral universe that most people inhabit, Sal and Dean are beyond accountability. For instance, in *Visions of Cody*, Kerouac imagines that Cassady has merrily joined with the Three Stooges and concludes, "[A]ll the goofs he felt in him were justified in the outside world and he had nothing to reproach himself for" (1972, 306).

Turner elaborates on the significance of the substanceless state found in liminality:

> A further structurally negative characteristic of transitional beings is that they have nothing. They have no status, property, insignia, secular clothing, rank, kinship position, nothing to demarcate them structurally from their fellows. . . . In the words of King Lear they represent "naked unaccommodated man." (1967, 99)

This is a state toward which Sal strives: he attempts to leave the world of things. He literally has nothing; when Sal is not traveling he is living with his aunt, and she often sends him money to help him out of tight spots. Even Kerouac avoided association with most of the things that Turner lists above. He was an unobtrusive man who seemed to fit nowhere and yet who, at least for a while, was everywhere. Kerouac can be read to reject rank and social status as much as he rejects authority.

Sal's self-knowledge of his liminal position is suggested periodically when he pauses long enough from his ceaseless wandering to examine critically the implications of his and his group's lifestyle. This is most obvious when Dean shows up one day with photographs chronicling a recent adventure. Sal is struck by the contrast between what the photographs suggest and the actuality of their lives:

> I realized that these were all the snapshots which our children would look at someday with wonder, thinking their parents had lived smooth, well-ordered, stabilized-within-the-photo lives and got up in the morning to walk proudly on the sidewalks of life, never dreaming the raggedy madness and riot of our actual lives, our actual night, the hell of it, the senseless emptiness. (1957, 208)

This "hell" and the "senseless emptiness" is indicative of Kerouac's rhetorical vision when extended to the excesses of its ultimate position.

Pressed to their limits, the visions become abusive and ruinous and fall apart in the disparity between the ideal world of a seldom-maintained euphoria, on the one hand, and the constrictions of the larger social system, on the other. In this sense, Kerouac's experience serves as a microcosm for the larger cultural experiences of the decade that followed him.

The condition of liminality accentuates unhealthy traits in a social community. For example, Sarah Gilead implies that the liminal experience has its reactionary elements: similar to Aristotle's theory of catharsis, the liminal experience may circumvent unrest and social dissidence by using fantasy to help people reconcile themselves to contradictions found within the dominant reality:

> Seeming to be outside the group, the liminal figure is actually its moral representative and, in fact, exists to serve the social structure from which he seems to have been separated. The liminal figure provides for his audience a vicarious experience that offers a kind of safety valve for the hostility or frustration engendered by the limitations of structured life. . . . But the existence of that game-space, separated from the scene of power-seeking, role-playing, delimited self-definition, actually strengthens structure by satisfying egalitarian or other unstructured (or antistructured) longings with the game-space. . . . Social rules, categories, classes, and institutions are strengthened by enacting a fantasy of their weakness. (1986, 184)

For Gilead, liminality is an important force in empowering the literature-society dialectic, particularly those books that serve "as a culture-regenerating force in a bereft, conflicted society, a society that in itself is at a critical juncture, a risky threshold of change" (1987, 303), as was American society in the late 1950s and 1960s. As Gilead suggests, the liminal experience may not always be revolutionary; however, it is always transformational. What results from that transformation cannot be adequately classified as "good" or "bad"; rather, the liminal state offers an individual as well as a society the chance to recreate—always a risky process.[4]

Thus, the limitations of the liminal experience should not undermine the important role that liminality plays in culture. Indeed, the liminal experience is both a positive and negative construct for the visionary and for society. Turner makes the point that while the liminal position exists as a structural simplicity, it is "offset by its cultural complexity" (1967, 102). Turner cites several characters from folk literature and illustrates that their marginality, while problematic interpersonally, has larger and more productive societal implications. For example, he argues that the fugitive slave Jim in *Huckleberry Finn* and the prostitute Sonya in *Crime and Punishment*, along with more generic images of "holy beggars," "third sons," and "simpletons," are instances of "[s]ymbolic figures . . . who strip off the pretentiousness of holders of high rank and office and reduce them to the levels of common humanity and mortality" (1969, 110).

While the cost of liminality may be high for the individual, as in the case of Kerouac and Cassady or Sal and Dean, the potential of the liminal figure for cultural contribution is great. In this positive capacity, *On the Road* articulates an important cultural space for redescription and change. Liminality, which aided in the creation of the text, extended outside of the text to affect the larger subgroup of the Beats, hippies, and other sympathetic people through, in part, the self-sacrificial position of Kerouac, the group's visionary.

Kerouac's liminal position is accentuated by the fact that "mythic types are structurally inferior or 'marginal'" (Turner 1969, 111). In other words, the experience of liminal individuals is subservient to the social hierarchy in terms of status and class; however, these people or symbols represent an openness as opposed to a closedness in morality, "the latter being essentially the normative system of bounded, structured, particularistic groups" (1969, 110). In effect, the visionary serves as a catalyst for change. *On the Road* is an important statement of that catalyst, and the fantasy themes found in the drama make the story appealing to readers who are encouraged by the larger world vision Kerouac is prompting. Kerouac's rhetorical vision is an extension of his self-sacrificial effort to modify social reality. Most important, the primary advantage of liminality in the *On the Road* drama is its ability to shed light on the human condition. As Turner remarks, "In closed or structured societies, it is the marginal or 'inferior' person or the 'outsider' who often comes to symbolize what David Hume called 'the sentiment for humanity'" (1969, 111).

Dennis McNally stresses the importance liminality plays in the historical relevance of the Beat Generation. McNally connects the "marginal" person, embodying a socially significant sentimentality, with key cultural figures of post–World War II America (such as Kerouac, Cassady, and the crowd of artists that surrounded them). He explains, "In a world that faces a potential ecological and spiritual apocalypse, I respectfully submit that the legend of these psychic pioneers is necessary in order that we might [better] understand our present reality" (1979, ix). In McNally's observation we find a socially significant justification for a study such as this one and other inquiries into Kerouac's world.

As suggested, liminality plays an important role in Kerouac's experience, offering him the perceptions of the world that later make their way into his fiction. With his understanding of the human condition, Kerouac makes judgments based on that experience and shares those judgments with a larger audience. For example, the three fantasy themes of social deviance, sexuality, and Dean represent Kerouac's attempt to bridge the gap between his personal experience of the human condition (his private vision) and the reality found in the dominant culture around him.

Furthermore, knowledge of the liminal experience adds depth to this study by helping to explain the basic psyche of Kerouac. Nicosia notes that Kerouac "spent his life proving that the past is the root of the future, and that man cannot live without the continuity of both" (1994, 21). Ironically, Kerouac's troubled life indicates that he was not able to draw strength from the past or the future, that he belonged to neither world and had clung, detrimentally, to the liminal state. Nicosia adds that Kerouac "was a man for whom nothing was secure, not even his name" (1994, 21).

Toward the end of their travels together, Sal and Dean find themselves among the poverty-stricken residents of Mexico City. Here, among the brothels, barefooted old women, and simple meals, Sal notices that "[b]eggars slept wrapped in advertising posters torn off fences" (1957, 248). The symbolism of this image is intriguing: similar images appear in the naturalist novels of Theodore Dreiser (1927) and Upton Sinclair (1906), but they take on an entirely different tone in Kerouac's romanticism. In the midst of his excitement, Sal declares, "This was the great and final uninhibited Fellahin-childlike city that we knew we would find at the end of the road" (1957, 248). Rather than recoil at the horrors of poverty, as Dreiser and Sinclair did, Sal is ecstatic: he had found a world where people could live in simplicity as unadorned and non-materially driven citizens. The sleeping beggars and the peasants who use newspapers for plates represent a message that people can make do with what is provided naturally; even in the city where fences and walls have replaced rivers and trees, this basic sentiment still applies. Kerouac reminds his readers that in spite of twentieth-century pretentiousness, people are still human.

The idealistic message of Kerouac's fantasy is a counterstatement to the negativism and corruption of the corporate fantasy that America disseminates. The conflict between the two interests continues to be played out. The responsibility of the reader is to chart the tension caused by this conflict by highlighting what is implicit in the dialectic between Kerouac's text and the evolving needs of our contemporary historical contingencies. The conflict in values that *On the Road* exemplifies has a real presence for us; a brutal conservatism and intolerance, one that has always been a part of the American political landscape, is asserting itself in increasingly dominant ways.

When examining the fantasy themes of a novel, the reader is able to analyze the rhetorical visions of its author. In particular, this study of *On the Road* produces noteworthy observations regarding the structure of

Kerouac's rhetorical vision. First, Kerouac's novel significantly influenced American culture because it introduces and promotes an alternative social reality (at the very least it represents a subversive cultural style). Second, the fantasy themes that promote this vision extend far beyond the text and into culture. Therefore, by placing the work in its cultural context, the reader is further able to explore the effects of the rhetorical vision on society.

Kerouac's vision, in particular, is a historically important construct to evaluate, and *On the Road* is a central artifact of this country's counterculture. Ronald J. Oakley reminds readers that Kerouac's novel "expressed [a] yearning for freedom and meaning in the last years of the Eisenhower era" (1986, 399). Oakley notes the effects of this expression as having raised "a valuable voice of protest against America's consumer culture that was heard and even heeded by a few" (402). Because Kerouac was able to accomplish what Oakley describes, both the vision and the artifact deserve research attention.

The effects of Kerouac and *On the Road*, as argued in part 1, imply an alternative experience to the dominant culture. Charters notes that *On the Road* exceeds its role as literature and becomes an invitation for "adventure": "[Young people] recognized that Kerouac was on their side, the side of youth and freedom, riding with Cassady over American highways chasing after the great American adventure—freedom and open spaces, the chance to be yourself, to be free" (1973, 288). More specifically, Nicosia illustrates one way in which Kerouac's alternative experience made a difference in American life: "Kerouac's greatest impact was on the millions of kids . . . who read *On the Road* . . . and suddenly realized that there was more to the world than their own small town" (1984, 4). Furthermore, Kerouac's influence is "lasting" because it extends beyond his own life to today's readers by virtue of *On the Road*'s more than forty years of continuous publication. More important than the contemporary presence of the text, Kerouac's rhetorical vision continues to exist in a muted but sometimes discernible fashion. As noted earlier, aspects of Kerouac's rhetorical vision can be seen in the growing concern for ecology and cooperative business, for example. As long as remnants of the 1960s experience remain, Kerouac's vision will remain, long after his name ceases to have any cultural resonance. In other words, Kerouac helped create an experience that is larger than himself.

This study has only scratched the surface of a significant cultural discourse. Further inquiry is necessary to establish a greater understanding of Kerouac's role as a rhetorician in articulating a consciousness in post-World War II America. While little more than an initial step in understanding a vastly intricate rhetorical phenomenon, my study has practical implications for individuals interested in the sub- and countercultures of the 1950s and 1960s. For instance, a study such as this may help explain the peculiar relationship between a writer such as Kerouac and the expectations of his audience. As Barry Gifford and Lawrence Lee note:

> America makes odd demands of its fiction writers. Their art alone won't do. We expect them to provide us with social stencils, an expectation so firm that we often judge their lives instead of their works. If they declare themselves a formal movement or stand up together as a generation, we are pleased, because this simplifies the use we plan to make of them. (1978, prologue)

In another age, Kerouac might have been honored as a rhapsode for his poetic contributions to culture. However, he has been widely criticized as a social anomaly and destructive force in culture. In a sense, he has been condemned as a sophist for corrupting the youth with his promotion of a hedonistic nihilism. This study has attempted to refigure that negative image of Kerouac by identifying him as a cultural rhetorician, capable of promoting and sustaining a message deliberately designed to modify social reality.

Notes
Bibliography
Index

Notes

1. Rhetorical Transformations

1. Kuhn (1970) explains how paradigms create the conditions under which discipline-dependent knowledge can be known. His discussion serves as a model for describing the function of vision-dependent ideology in the construction of our social lives.

2. As a critic, I am empathetic to the world that Kerouac constructs, and I recognize—indeed, celebrate—my partiality as a scholar in support of his project as well as in support of the visions of resistance by others still to come.

3. Cassady is portrayed in *On the Road* as the protagonist Dean Moriarty. The Merry Pranksters were prototypical hippies that emerged around Ken Kesey in Palo Alto as the result of secret CIA LSD testing in the early to mid-1960s. The Merry Pranksters included the young Jerry Garcia and others who formed the Grateful Dead and provided music for the "acid tests," public mass LSD parties that took place in different cities throughout the United States. LSD was legal until 1966. For a discussion of the Cassady/Kesey/acid/CIA connection, see Lee and Shlain (1985).

4. These three albums have been repackaged and remastered and appear under the Rhino label in a CD box set entitled *The Jack Kerouac Collection* (1990).

5. Deleuze and Guattari write that people like Kerouac "overcome a limit, they shatter a wall, the capitalist barrier" (1983, 133). Nevertheless, Deleuze and Guattari offer a dim view of Kerouac, hinting that there is something oppressive and potentially fascist in his "revolutionary 'flight'" (1983, 277).

6. When Burke discusses piety, what he calls a "schema of orientation,"

he writes, "[L]ife has been likened to the writing of a poem, though some people write their poems on paper, and others carve theirs out of jugular veins" (1984, 76). For a larger discussion of piety in Burke's work, see Rosteck and Leff (1989).

Kerouac and Ginsberg romanticize Cassady as a poet of the highest order and claim that he inspired them to create their work.

2. Kerouac in Context

1. City Lights Books, founded in 1953, was the first paperback book store in the country and was devoted to publishing Beat authors.

2. While northern California was a central place of countercultural activity, it was not the only place in America where communes and other ideological activity took place. See Berger (1981).

3. Not all of his work was published during or around this time, however. For instance, *Visions of Cody* was not published until after his death. In the 1990s, interest in Kerouac, spawned in great deal by the efforts of Charters to revive him, has led to the publication of some of his unpublished writings (1992, 1993, 1995a, 1995b, 1995c). A second major reason for the spate of new Kerouac material involves the 1990 death of Stella Kerouac (Jack Kerouac's third wife). Stella was hostile to the literary world, which she blamed for Kerouac's troubles, and she suppressed her late husband's unpublished manuscripts for over twenty years.

4. Kerouac's other "road" books, such as *The Subterraneans* (1958c), *Big Sur* (1962), and *The Dharma Bums* (1958b), do not focus on Neal Cassady (although he does play a part in most of them).

5. See Stimpson (1982) for a study of homosexuality among the major writers in Beat culture.

6. This is a particularly evident theme in much of Ginsberg's poetry. See, for instance, Ginsberg's homage to Cassady's penis, a poem entitled "Done, Finished with the Biggest Cock" (1984, 466).

7. See Chomsky (1994) for a contemporary appraisal of what he identifies as American hypocrisy and political repression.

8. God, in fact, appears or is evoked frequently in the text and is usually associated with the road, as exemplified in Kerouac's phrase "[T]he road is life" (1957, 175). Kerouac's God is Western-looking: he is an old man with a white-streaked beard and hair who walks on the road. This God even becomes embodied in Dean, as when Kerouac writes, "I had to struggle to see Dean's figure, and he looked like God" (1957, 233).

9. For a men's studies approach to issues of fatherhood in Kerouac's writings, see Davenport (1992).

10. For a selection of Beat writing on Buddhism, see Tonkinson (1995).

11. The real-life Herbert Huncke and Bill Cannastra, as well as the

fictional Mardou in *The Subterraneans*, are also examples of liminal figures in Kerouac's world.

12. This lifestyle did have its literary genesis, in part, elsewhere. Perhaps it is clearer to write that Kerouac did not "invent" a new lifestyle; rather, he updated an older one by reading the works of Rimbaud, Celine, and Gide. Kerouac is but a participant in a long tradition of bohemianism who served the important function of popularizing, through his writing, countercultural themes (see Riesman 1961; Goodman 1960; and Ehrenreich 1983).

13. The clearest articulation of Kerouac's position as patriarch is *On the Road*, the book that "captured the spirit of [Kerouac's] generation, their restlessness and confusions in the years immediately following World War II." Charters summarizes this perspective by writing, "[P]eople looked at Kerouac as if *he* were the Beat Generation" (1973, 297).

14. Oakley explains that the Beats "were the progenitors of the hippies, yippies, and other youthful members of the counter-culture of the sixties" (1986, 402).

15. This is not to imply that the two groups can be reduced to a seamless whole. With continuity also comes disjunction and even antagonism (see Rather 1977).

3. Kerouac's Rhetorical Situation

1. Rhetoric is, first and foremost, a perspective. Perspectives make sense only when viewed from a specific location. As a perspective, rhetoric is not "real" in the sense that we can find a rhetorical "fossil" embedded in a text, as we find fossils of clams and mussels embedded in rocks. Rather, rhetorical "fossils" are shadows that involve both light and darkness, clear passages and blockages. Shadows, like rhetoric, make sense, in fact, can be seen, only from a certain perspective. Texts such as *On the Road* cast shadows: that is, they cast light as well as darkness. From far away we can see the contours of the mountains in the sky; their shadows are reflected in the clouds during the sunset. Readers can learn to see the same things in cultural artifacts.

2. Methods help to historicize a scholar and his or her writing. History is the plateau on which we stand to view the mountain, or text, that we wish to study. In the case of this book, fantasy theme criticism is the specific lens that I have chosen to attach to my telescope to study the fine detail of the "mountain" about which I have chosen to write. However, texts are not like mountains in some important aspects. Critics and readers, or scientists as the case may be, are limited in how they approach their relationship to a mountain. A scientist may seek to *understand* the mountain—where it came from, where it is going, what it is made of, and

how it can be used by people. In addition to being understood, a mountain can be *appreciated*. It may be perceived as being either beautiful or ugly; it may lend itself to painting or sculpture; it may inspire poetry or philosophy. In contemplating a mountain, a person usually cannot be a critic. Mountains are not judged. They cannot be symbolically modified. They are not themselves symbols (although people can certainly turn them into symbols).

When faced with a text, the critic goes beyond what the scientist or the artist can do. The critic is not only interested in understanding or appreciating an artifact. Rather, critics engage with texts in ways that differ from the manner in which geologists engage with mountains. Texts are more flexible than mountains: they change in small ways with each reading. Their power to inform, influence, and persuade grows and diminishes with each analysis. Certainly, texts do not need professional critics to accomplish their social work; but professional criticism helps. In small ways, critics inform texts, texts inform critics, and both contribute to a reading audience in ways that are, likewise, transformational.

3. Granted, Chomsky is a controversial figure. Nevertheless, his arguments need to be debated, not ignored or spurned because people do not like to hear what he has to say. For an overview of Chomsky's critique of the United States and its foreign policy, see Rai (1995) and Barsky (1997).

4. Nicosia reports that Kerouac was kicked out of the Navy when he threw down his rifle, stubbornly refusing to carry a weapon (1994, 104).

5. Podhoretz defended Israel's invasion of Lebanon in 1982 as well as the massacres of Arabs that followed. He wrote, "[T]he people of Lebanon were overjoyed at being liberated from PLO domination and tyranny" (1982, A27). Furthermore, he claimed that criticism of the Israeli invasion and subsequent occupation was a sign of anti-Semitism.

6. This is one of Chomsky's (1989) theses about how thought control works in U.S. society. According to Chomsky, opinion leaders reinforce the dominant ideology that the government promotes as a "state religion." Thought control, in effect, is designed to stifle thought and keep alternative ideas or questions from arising (Lester 1992). Thus, state ideologues such as Podhoretz are dangerous for democracy. Chomsky is very clear in his writing that the "criminal" policies of the United States have been successful in part because of ideologues such as Podhoretz (for the most clear example of this, see Chomsky 1967). Likewise, by encouraging alternative or dissident thought, writers such as Kerouac are dangerous to the undemocratic state. Thus we find that the efforts of state ideologues are often directed at discrediting those thinkers who challenge state orthodoxy.

7. Had John bought a new copy of *On the Road*, it would have been an admission on the part of Volvo that the book has relevant social messages for the present. In addition, by relegating *On the Road* to the attic, Volvo implies that it is a relic, hidden away without any relevance besides nostalgia.

8. Lest we forget, Huxley's "brave new world" is not so brave, not so new, and not so much his imagination. Indeed, as Neil Postman reminds us, the tyranny we have to face in our culture may not be the one that George Orwell (1949) warned us about, but the one that Huxley did (1985, vii–viii). Also, see Parenti (1993, 24–25).

9. As a child, Kerouac had been raised in a Republican home, so there is a sense in which he is simply returning to his roots.

4. Fantasy, Rhetorical Vision, and the Critical Act

1. "Vision," it should be noted, is being used in two senses. In its larger sense, Kerouac's rhetorical vision refers to his global, epistemic position. Visions in this encompassing sense are paradigmatic. In its more localized sense, "vision" refers to specific descriptions of social deviance, sexuality, and Dean (as an agent of transcendence). In other words, each specific vision is a fantasy theme, a small-*v* vision that summatively represents the larger epistemology.

2. Indeed, this is Foucault's basic methodology (1972). For a discussion of his methodology and its relationship to culture, ideology, and criticism, see Swartz (1997, chapter 2).

3. For a discussion of ideology, see Eagleton (1991).

4. Reading traditional art forms, or poetics, in terms of rhetorical discourse is made feasible by Kenneth Burke. For a detailed discussion of this, see Swartz (1996a).

5. The Vision of Social Deviance

1. More obviously, "Sal" is Latin for "salt" (as in "salt of the earth") and Salvadore, Sal's proper name, is Italian for "savior."

2. Specifically, Kerouac's style is an example of "foregrounding." For a discussion of foregrounding, see Leech and Short (1981, 28).

3. This argumentative tactic is exemplified in the discourse of J. Edgar Hoover. See Swartz (1996c) for a specific study.

4. While this claim has theoretical and intuitive integrity, it is true that Kerouac personally expressed contrary behaviors at times.

5. Primeau (1996) places Kerouac's novel in the history of road narratives and argues that *On the Road* defines the genre in the United States.

6. The complexities of "ideology," as a concept, is the subject of much

critical theory. For a selective overview of critical theory, see Bronner and Kellner (1989).

7. See Walker (1980) for a discussion of police corruption in U.S. history.

6. The Vision of Sexuality

1. Kerouac is not the only person to discuss sexuality in a way that suggests its socially constructed character (see Foucault 1978).

2. Regardless of what larger social effects may have occurred as the result of Kerouac's Vision of Sexuality and the larger vision of sexuality that received much attention in the late 1960s, one thing is clear: many women were raped in the name of "free love."

3. Kerouac's condescending attitude toward the *fellahin* that he so much romanticizes has been noted by Holton, who writes, "Kerouac's ethnic others rarely emerge from a sort of pastoral (or urban-pastoral) simplicity" (1995, 270).

4. This is an allusion to William Carlos Williams's book-length poem *Paterson* (1946).

5. For a racial/gender/economic critique of representations of minorities in popular culture, see bell hooks (1992, 1994).

7. Dean as Vision

1. For a sophisticated review of the philosophical and critical dimensions of metaphor, see Moran (1989).

2. Kerouac's books of reminiscence differ from his "road" books in that they focus on his romantic memories of childhood and do not describe the antics of the Beat Generation.

8. Conclusion: Kerouac and Liminality

1. For his elucidation of neopragmatism, see Rorty (1982).

2. There is a precedent for applying liminality to the study of literature; see Firmat (1986); Gilead (1986, 1987); Greenstein (1990); and Walker (1987). In communication studies, the concept has been utilized in conjunction with much ethnographic research, particularly in the work of Conquergood (1989, 1991) and Katriel (1991). For a recent study of liminality in rhetorical criticism, see Morris (1996).

3. In a sense, Kerouac and Cassady belong to a cult of death. This "cult" is best exemplified by its illustrious members—Jim Morrison, Jimi Hendrix, and Janis Joplin—but includes thousands of nameless people who destroyed their lives in pursuit of a transcendence derived through chemical dependency.

4. Didion (1968) clearly describes the risk involved in a liminal culture's moral development. Her ambivalence toward the social project of the hippies is best summed up in the title of her essay, "Slouching Toward Bethlehem."

Bibliography

Alberts, J. K. 1986. "The Role of Couple's Conversations in Relational Development: A Content Analysis of Courtship Talk in Harlequin Romance Novels." *Communication Quarterly* 34: 127–42.

Anctil, Pierre. 1990. Preface to *Un Homme Grand: Jack Kerouac at the Crossroads of Many Cultures*, ed. Pierre Anctil, Louis Dupont, Remi Ferland, and Eric Waddell. Ottawa: Carleton University Press. xviii–xix.

Backman, Mark. 1991. *Sophistication: Rhetoric and the Rise of Self-Consciousness*. Woodbridge, CN: Oxbow.

Bales, Robert F. 1970. *Personality and Interpersonal Behavior*. New York: Holt, Rinehart and Winston.

Baraka, Amiri. 1963. *Blues People: The Negro Experience in White America and Music That Developed from It*. New York: Morrow.

Barsky, Robert F. 1997. *Noam Chomsky: A Life of Dissent*. Cambridge, MA: MIT Press.

Barthes, Roland. 1972. *Mythologies*. New York: Noonday.

Berger, Bennett M. 1981. *The Survival of a Counterculture: Ideological Work and Everyday Life among Rural Communards*. Berkeley: University of California Press.

Berrigan, Ted. 1968. "The Art of Fiction LXI: Jack Kerouac." *Paris Review* 43: 60–105.

Berry, Mary Francis, and John Blassingame. 1982. *Long Memory: The Black Experience in America*. New York: Oxford University Press.

Bhabba, Homi K. 1994. *The Location of Culture*. New York: Routledge.

Bird, William. 1989. "Enterprise and Meaning: Sponsored Film, 1939–1949." *History Today* 39: 24–30.

Black, Edwin. 1980. "A Note on Theory and Practice in Rhetorical Criticism." *Western Journal of Speech Communication* 44: 331–36.

Blackstock, Nelson. 1988. *COINTELPRO: The FBI's Secret War on Political Freedom*. New York: Pathfinder.

Bormann, Ernest G. 1972. "Fantasy and Rhetorical Vision: The Rhetorical Criticism of Social Reality." *Quarterly Journal of Speech* 58: 394–407.

———. 1982. "Fantasy and Rhetorical Vision: Ten Years Later." *Quarterly Journal of Speech* 68: 288–305.

———. 1983. "Symbolic Convergence: Organizational Communication and Culture." In *Communication and Organizations: An Interpretative Approach*, ed. Linda L. Putnam and Michael E. Pacanowsky. Beverly Hills: Sage. 99–122.

———. 1985. *The Force of Fantasy: Restoring the American Dream*. Carbondale: Southern Illinois University Press.

Bormann, Ernest G., John F. Cragan, and Donald C. Shields. 1994. "In Defense of Symbolic Convergence Theory: A Look at the Theory and Its Criticisms after Two Decades." *Communication Theory* 4: 259–94.

Bormann, Ernest G., John F. Cragan, Donald C. Shields, and Yoshihisa Itaba. 1992. "Why Do People Share Fantasies? An Empirical Investigation of a Basic Tenet of the Symbolic Convergence Theory in a Sample of Japanese Subjects." *Human Communication Studies* 20: 1–25.

Bowers, John Waite, and Donovan J. Ochs. 1971. *The Rhetoric of Agitation and Control*. Menlo Park, CA: Addison-Wesley.

Bridges, Bill. 1996. "Logology." In *Encyclopedia of Rhetoric and Composition*, ed. Theresa Enos. New York: Garland Publishing. 409–10.

Brock, Bernard L., Robert L. Scott, and James W. Chesebro. 1990. *Methods of Rhetorical Criticism: A Twentieth-Century Perspective*. 3rd ed. Detroit: Wayne State University Press.

Bronner, Stephen, and Douglas Kellner, eds. 1989. *Critical Theory and Society: A Reader*. New York: Routledge.

Buchanan, Richard. 1996. "Richard P. McKeon (1900–1985)." In *Encyclopedia of Rhetoric and Composition*, ed. Theresa Enos. New York: Garland Publishing. 424–28.

Burke, Kenneth. 1966. *Language as Symbolic Action*. Berkeley: University of California Press.

———. 1969a. *A Grammar of Motives*. 1945. Reprint, Berkeley: University of California Press.

———. 1969b. *A Rhetoric of Motives*. 1950. Reprint, Berkeley: University of California Press.

———. 1970. *Rhetoric of Religion*. 1961. Reprint, Berkeley: University of California Press.

———. 1972. *Dramatism and Development*. Barre, MA: Clark University Press.

———. 1973. *The Philosophy of Literary Form*. 1941. Reprint, Berkeley: University of California Press.

———. 1984. *Permanence and Change: An Anatomy of Purpose*. 1935. Reprint, Berkeley: University of California Press.

Campbell, Karlyn Kohrs, and Kathleen Jamieson. 1977. "Form and Genre in Rhetorical Criticism: An Introduction." In *Form and Genre: Shaping Rhetorical Action*, ed. Karlyn Kohrs Campbell and Kathleen Jamieson. Falls Church, VA: Speech Communication Association. 9–32.

Camus, Albert. 1991. *Between Hell and Reason: Essays from the Resistance Newspaper Combat, 1944–1947*. Hanover, NH: Wesleyan University Press.

Carey, Alex. 1997. *Taking the Risk out of Democracy*. Urbana: University of Illinois Press.

Carson, Rachel. 1962. *Silent Spring*. Boston: Houghton Mifflin.

Cassady, Neal. 1971. *The First Third and Other Writings*. San Francisco: City Lights.

———. 1993. *Grace Beats Karma: Letters from Prison, 1958–60*. New York: Blast.

Cassady, Neal, and Allen Ginsberg. 1977. *As Ever: The Collected Correspondence of Allen Ginsberg and Neal Cassady*. Berkeley: Creative Arts Book Co.

Cathcart, Robert. 1978. "Movements: Confrontation as Rhetorical Form." *Southern Speech Communication Journal* 43: 233–47.

Challis, Chris. 1984. *Quest for Kerouac*. London: Faber and Faber.

Charland, Maurice. 1987. "Constitutive Rhetoric: The Case of the *Peuple Quebecois*." *Quarterly Journal of Speech* 73: 133–50.

Charters, Ann. 1973. *Kerouac: A Biography*. San Francisco: Straight Arrow.

Chomsky, Noam. 1967. *American Power and the New Mandarins*. New York: Vintage.

———. 1983. *The Fateful Triangle: The United States, Israel, and the Palestinians*. Boston: South End.

———. 1988. *The Culture of Terrorism*. Boston: South End.

———. 1989. *Necessary Illusions: Thought Control in Democratic Societies*. Boston: South End.

———. 1994. *Keeping the Rabble in Line: Interviews with David Barsamin*. Monroe, ME: Common Courage.

Chomsky, Noam, and Edward S. Herman. 1979. *The Washington Connection and Third World Fascism*. Boston: South End.

Churchill, Ward, and Jim Vander Wall. 1988. *Agents of Repression: The FBI's Secret Wars Against the Black Panther Party and the American Indian Movement*. Boston: South End.

———. 1990. *The COINTELPRO Papers: Documents from the FBI's Secret Wars Against Domestic Dissent.* Boston: South End.

Clark, Tom. 1984. *Jack Kerouac.* New York: Harcourt.

Clinton, Bill. 1993. "Inaugural Address." *Weekly Compilation of Presidential Documents* 29: 75–77.

———. 1994. Proclamation 6680. *Federal Register* 59 (30 Apr.): 22957.

Conquergood, Dwight. 1989. "Poetics, Process, and Power: The Performative Turn in Anthropology." *Text and Performance Quarterly* 9: 82–98.

———. 1991. "Rethinking Ethnography: Towards a Critical Cultural Politics." *Communication Monographs* 58: 179–94.

Cook, Bruce. 1971. *The Beat Generation.* New York: Charles Scribner's Sons.

Davenport, Steve. 1992. "Complicating 'A Very Masculine Aesthetic': Positional Sons and Double Husbands, Kinship and Careening in Jack Kerouac's Fiction." Ph.d. diss., University of Illinois, Urbana.

Davidson, Michael. 1989. *The San Francisco Renaissance: Poetics and Community at Mid-Century.* New York: Cambridge University Press.

de Certeau, Michel. 1984. *The Practice of Everyday Life.* Berkeley: University of California Press.

Deleuze, Gilles, and Felix Guattari. 1983. *Anti-Oedipus: Capitalism and Schizophrenia.* Minneapolis: University of Minnesota Press.

Didion, Joan. 1968. "Slouching Toward Bethlehem." In *Slouching Toward Bethlehem.* New York: Farrar, Straus, and Giroux. 84–128.

Directory of National Biography 18. 1921. London: Oxford University Press.

Doyle, Marsha Vanderford. 1985. "The Rhetoric of Romance: A Fantasy Theme Analysis of Barbara Cartland Novels." *Southern Speech Communication Journal* 51: 24–49.

Dreiser, Theodore. 1927. *Sister Carrie.* Cleveland: World Publishing.

Eagleton, Terry. 1991. *Ideology: An Introduction.* London: Verso.

Ehrenreich, Barbara. 1983. *The Hearts of Men: American Dreams and the Flight from Commitment.* Garden City, NY: Anchor.

Enos, Richard Leo. 1978. "The Hellenic Rhapsode." *Western Journal of Speech Communication* 42: 134–43.

Ferlinghetti, Lawrence. 1976. *Howl of the Censors.* Westport, CT: Greenwood.

Finney, Jack. 1955. *Invasion of the Body Snatchers.* New York: Dell.

Firmat, Gustavo Perez. 1986. *Literature and Liminality: Festive Readings in the Hispanic Tradition.* Durham, NC: Duke University Press.

Fisher, Walter. 1987. *Human Communication as Narration: Toward a Philosophy of Reason, Value, and Action.* Columbia: University of South Carolina Press.

Foucault, Michel. 1970. *The Order of Things: An Archaeology of the Human Sciences*. New York: Vintage.

———. 1972. *The Archaeology of Knowledge*. New York: Pantheon.

———. 1977. *Discipline and Punish*. New York: Vintage.

———. 1978. *History of Sexuality*. New York: Vintage.

———. 1980. *Power/Knowledge*. New York: Pantheon.

Fyne, Robert. 1985. "From Hollywood to Moscow." *Literature and Film Quarterly* 13: 194–99.

Gennep, Arnold van. 1960. *The Rites of Passage*. London: Routledge and Kegan Paul.

George, Paul, and Jerold M. Starr. 1985. "Beat Politics: New Left and Hippie Beginnings in the Postwar Counterculture." In *Cultural Politics: Radical Movements in Modern History*, ed. Jerold M. Starr. New York: Praeger. 189–234.

Gibson, Chester. 1970. "Eugene Talmadge's Use of Identification During the 1934 Gubernatorial Campaign in Georgia." *Southern Speech Journal* 35: 342–49.

Gifford, Barry, and Lawrence Lee. 1978. *Jack's Book: An Oral Biography of Jack Kerouac*. New York: St. Martin's.

Gilead, Sarah. 1986. "Liminality, Anti-Liminality, and the Victorian Novel." *Journal of English Literary History* 53: 183–97.

———. 1987. "Liminality and Anti-Liminality in Charlotte Brontë's Novels: Shirley Reads *Jane Eyre*." *Texas Studies in Language and Literature* 29: 302–22.

Ginsberg, Allen. 1972. Introduction to *Visions of Cody*, by Jack Kerouac. New York: McGraw-Hill. vii–xii.

———. 1984. *Collected Poems: 1947–1980*. New York: Harper and Row.

Goodman, Paul. 1960. *Growing Up Absurd: Problems of Youth in the Organized Society*. New York: Vintage.

Greenstein, Michael. 1990. "Liminality in *Little Dorrit*." *Dickens Quarterly* 7: 275–83.

Gregg, Richard B. 1984. *Symbolic Inducement and Knowing*. Columbia: University of South Carolina Press.

Gronbeck, Bruce E. 1980. "Dramaturgical Theory and Criticism: The State of the Art (or Science?)." *Western Journal of Speech Communication* 44: 315–30.

Gross, Bertram. 1980. *Friendly Fascism: The New Face of Power in America*. Boston: South End.

Hart, Roderick P. 1990. *Modern Rhetorical Criticism*. Glenview: Scott, Foresman and Company.

Herman, Edward S., and Noam Chomsky. 1988. *Manufacturing Consent: The Political Economy of the Mass Media*. New York: Pantheon.

Holmes, John Clellon. 1952. "This Is the Beat Generation." *New York Times Magazine* 16 Nov., 10.

———. 1967. *Nothing More to Declare*. New York: E. P. Dutton.

Holton, Robert. 1995. "Kerouac among the *Fellahin*: On the Road to the Postmodern." *Modern Fiction Studies* 41: 265–83.

hooks, bell. 1992. *Black Looks: Race and Representation*. Boston: South End.

———. 1994. *Outlaw Culture: Resisting Representations*. New York: Routledge.

Hubbard, Rita C. 1985. "Relationship Styles in Popular Romance Novels: 1950 to 1983." *Communication Quarterly* 33: 113–25.

Hunt, Tim. 1981. *Kerouac's Crooked Road: Development of a Fiction*. Hamden, CT: Archon.

Huxley, Aldous. 1969. *Brave New World*. 1932. Reprint, New York: Harper and Row.

Jackson, Carl T. 1988. "The Counterculture Looks East: Beat Writers and Asian Religion." *American Studies* 29: 51–70.

James, William. 1985. *Varieties of Religious Experience*. 1902. Reprint, Cambridge, MA: Harvard University Press.

Johnson, Glen M. 1979. "'We'd Fight. . . . We Had To.' *The Body Snatchers* as Novel and Film." *Journal of Popular Culture* 13: 5–14.

Johnson, Joyce. 1983. *Minor Characters*. Boston: Houghton Mifflin.

Jones, James T. 1992. *A Map of Mexico City Blues: Jack Kerouac as Poet*. Carbondale: Southern Illinois University Press.

Katriel, Tamar. 1991. *Communication Webs: Communication and Culture in Contemporary Israel*. Albany: State University of New York Press.

Kerouac, Jack. 1957. *On the Road*. New York: Viking.

———. 1958a. *The Dharma Bums*. New York: Viking.

———. 1958b. *Dr. Sax*. New York: Grove.

———. 1958c. *The Subterraneans*. New York: Grove.

———. 1959a. *Maggie Cassady*. New York: Avon.

———. 1959b. *Mexico City Blues*. New York: Grove.

———. 1960. *The Scripture of the Golden Eternity*. New York: Cornity.

———. 1962. *Big Sur*. New York: Farrar, Straus and Cudahy.

———. 1963. *Visions of Gerard*. New York: Farrar, Straus and Company.

———. 1972. *Visions of Cody*. New York: McGraw-Hill.

———. 1992. *Poems All Sizes*. San Francisco: City Lights.

———. 1993. *Good Blonde and Other Stories*. San Francisco: Gray Fox.

———. 1995a. *The Portable Jack Kerouac*. New York: Viking.

———. 1995b. *Selected Letters 1948–1956*. New York: Viking.

———. 1995c. *Some of the Dharma*. New York: Viking.

Kherdian, David. 1967. *Six Poets of the San Francisco Renaissance:*

Portraits and Checklists. Fresno, CA: Giligia.

King, Martin Luther, Jr. 1968. *The Trumpet of Conscience.* New York: HarperCollins.

———. 1992. "I Have a Dream." In *I Have a Dream: Writing and Speeches That Changed the World.* Sunnyvale, CA: Scott-Foresman. 101–6.

Klehr, Harvey, and John Earl Haynes. 1992. *The American Communist Movement.* New York: Twayne.

Kuhn, Thomas S. 1970. *The Structure of Scientific Revolutions.* 2d ed. Chicago: University of Chicago Press.

Laclau, Ernesto, and Chantal Mouffe. 1985. *Hegemony and Socialist Strategy: Toward a Radical Democratic Politics.* London: Verso.

Lamont, Corliss. 1990. *Freedom Is as Freedom Does.* New York: Continuum.

Lauridsen, Inger Thorup, and Per Dalgard. 1990. *The Beat Generation and the Russian New Wave.* Ann Arbor: Ardis.

Lee, Martin A., and Bruce Shlain. 1985. *Acid Dreams: The CIA, LSD, and the Sixties Rebellion.* New York: Grove.

Leech, Geoffrey N., and Michael H. Short. 1981. *Style in Fiction: A Linguistic Introduction to English Fictional Prose.* New York: Longman.

Lester, Ellis. 1992. "Manufactured Silence and the Politics of Media Research: A Consideration of the Propaganda Model." *Journal of Communication Inquiry* 16: 45–55.

Mailer, Norman. 1958. "The White Negro." In *The Beat Generation and the Angry Young Men,* ed. Gene Feldman and Max Gartenberg. New York: Citadel. 342–63.

Marshall, Jonathan, Peter Dale Scott, and Jane Hunter. 1987. *The Iran-Contra Connection: Secret Teams and Covert Operations in the Reagan Era.* Boston: South End.

McGee, Michael C. 1975. "In Search of 'The People': A Rhetorical Alternative." *Quarterly Journal of Speech* 61: 235–49.

McNally, Dennis Sean. 1979. *Desolation Angel: Jack Kerouac, the Beat Generation, and America.* New York: Random House.

Mencken, H. L. 1994. *A Second Mencken Chrestomathy.* New York: Vintage.

Milewsky, Robert J. 1981. *Jack Kerouac: An Annotated Bibliography of Secondary Sources. 1944–1979.* Metuchen, NJ: Scarecrow.

Millstein, Gilbert. 1957. Review of *On the Road,* by Jack Kerouac. *New York Times,* 5 Sept., 34.

Mohrmann, G. P. 1980. "Elegy in a Critical Grave-Yard." *Western Journal of Speech Communication* 44: 265–74.

———. 1982a. "An Essay on Fantasy Theme Criticism." *Quarterly Journal of Speech* 68: 109–32.

———. 1982b. "Fantasy Theme Criticism: A Peroration." *Quarterly Journal of Speech* 68: 306–13.

Moran, Richard. 1989. "Seeing and Believing: Metaphor, Image, and Force." *Critical Inquiry* 16: 87–112.

Morris, Charles E., III. 1996. "Contextual Twilight/Critical Liminality: J. M. Varrie's *Courage* at St. Andrews, 1922." *Quarterly Journal of Speech* 82: 207–27.

Nicosia, Gerald. 1984. "Catching Up with Kerouac." In *Catching Up with Kerouac*, ed. V. J. Eaton. Phoenix: Literary Denim. 1–8.

———. 1994. *Memory Babe: A Critical Biography of Jack Kerouac.* Berkeley: University of California Press.

Oakley, Ronald J. 1986. *God's Country: America in the Fifties.* New York: Dembner.

Orwell, George. 1949. *1984, a Novel.* New York: Harcourt Brace.

Osborn, Michael. 1967. "Archetypal Metaphor in Rhetoric: The Ligh-Dark Family." *Quarterly Journal of Speech* 53: 115–26.

Panish, Jon. 1994. "Kerouac's *The Subterraneans*: A Study of 'Romantic Primitivism.'" *Melus* 19: 107–23.

Parenti, Michael. 1992. *Make-Believe Media: The Politics of Entertainment.* New York: St. Martin's.

———. 1993. *Inventing Reality: The Politics of the News Media.* New York: St. Martin's.

———. 1994. *Land of Idols: Political Mythology in America.* New York: St. Martin's.

Park, Douglas B. 1982. "The Meanings of 'Audience.'" *College English* 44: 247–57.

Perloff, Richard M. 1993. *The Dynamics of Persuasion.* Hillsdale, NJ: Lawrence Erlbaum.

Pike, Kenneth L. 1967. *Language in Relation to a Unified Theory of the Structure of Human Behavior.* 2d ed. Paris: Mouton.

Podhoretz, Norman. 1958. "The Know-Nothing Bohemians." *Partisan Review* 25: 305–18.

———. 1982. "The Massacre: Who Was Responsible?" *Washington Post* 24 Sept., A27.

Postman, Neil. 1985. *Amusing Ourselves to Death: Public Discourse in the Age of Show Business.* New York: Penguin.

Poulakos, Johan. 1984. "Rhetoric, the Sophists, and the Possible." *Communication Monographs* 51: 215–25.

Primeau, Ron. 1996. *Romance of the Road: The Literature of the American Highway.* Bowling Green, OH: Bowling Green State University Press.

Rai, Milan. 1995. *Chomsky's Politics.* New York: Verso.

Rao, Vimala C. 1974. "Oriental Influence on the Writings of Jack Kerouac, Allen Ginsberg, and Gary Snyder." Diss., University of Wisconsin.

Rather, Lois. 1977. *Bohemians to Hippies: Waves of Rebellion*. Oakland: Rather.

Rhino. 1990. Booklet accompanying *The Jack Kerouac Collection*. Sound recordings. Santa Monica, CA: Rhino.

Riesman, David. 1961. *The Lonely Crowd: A Study of the Changing American Character*. New Haven: Yale University Press.

Riordan, James, and Jerry Prochnicky. 1991. *Break on Through: The Life and Death of Jim Morrison*. New York: Morrow.

Rorty, Richard. 1979. *Philosophy and the Mirror of Nature*. Princeton: Princeton University Press.

———. 1982. *Consequences of Pragmatism*. Minneapolis: University of Minnesota Press.

———. 1989. *Contingency, Irony, and Solidarity*. Cambridge: Cambridge University Press.

———. 1991. *Essays on Heidegger and Others*. New York: Cambridge University Press.

Rosen, Ruth. 1986. "Search for Yesterday." In *Watching Television*, ed. Todd Gitlin. New York: Pantheon. 42–67.

Rosmarin, Adena. 1985. *The Power of Genre*. Minneapolis: University of Minnesota Press.

Rossiter, Clinton. 1962. *Conservatism in America*. 2d ed. New York: Vintage.

Rosteck, Thomas, and Michael Leff. 1989. "Piety, Propriety, and Perspective: An Interpretation and Application of Key Terms in Kenneth Burke's *Permanence and Change*." *Western Journal of Communication* 53: 327–41.

Said, Edward. 1978. *Orientalism*. London: Routledge and Kegan Paul.

Schiappa, Edward. 1992. "*Rhetorike*: What's in a Name? Toward a Revised History of Early Greek Rhetorical Theory." *Quarterly Journal of Speech* 78: 1–15.

Schwartz, Marilyn Merritt. 1976. "From Beat to Beatific: Religious Ideas in the Writings of Kerouac, Ginsberg, and Corso." Ph.D. diss., University of California, Davis.

Shields, Donald C. 1981. "A Dramatistic Approach to Applied Communication Research: Theory, Methods, and Applications." In *Applied Communication Research: A Dramatistic Approach*, ed. John F. Cragan and Donald C. Shields. Prospect Heights, IL: Waveland.

Sinclair, Upton. 1906. *The Jungle*. New York: Doubleday.

Sloan, De Villo. 1988. "The Self and Self-less in Campbell's *Who Goes There?* and Finney's *Invasion of the Body Snatchers*." *Extrapolation* 29: 179–88.

Smoodin, Eric. 1988. "Watching the Skies: Hollywood, the 1950s, and the Soviet Threat." *Journal of American Culture* 11: 35–40.

Sorrell, Richard. 1982. "The Catholicism of Jack Kerouac." *Studies in Religion* 11: 189–200.

Spengler, Oswald. 1926–1928. *The Decline of the West*. New York: A. A. Knopf.

Stauber, John, and Sheldon Rampton. 1995. *Toxic Sludge Is Good for You: Lies, Damn Lies, and the Public Relations Industry*. Monroe, ME: Common Courage.

Stein, Edward, ed. 1992. *Forms of Desire*. New York: Routledge.

Stephenson, Gregory. 1990. *The Daybreak Boys: Essays on the Literature of the Beat Generation*. Carbondale: Southern Illinois University Press.

Stewart, Charles J., Craig Allen Smith, and Robert E. Denton Jr. 1994. *Persuasion and Social Movements*. 3rd ed. Prospect Heights, IL: Waveland.

Stimpson, Catharine R. 1982. "The Beat Generation and the Trials of Homosexual Liberation." *Salmagundi* 58: 373–92.

Swartz, Omar. 1996a. "The 'Faith of Freedom' vs. The Freedom of Faith: Exploring the Totalitarian Discourse of J. Edgar Hoover." *Speaker and Gavel* 33: 59–73.

———. 1996b. "Kenneth Burke's Theory of Form: Rhetoric, Art, and Cultural Analysis." *Southern Communication Journal* 61: 312–21.

———. 1996c. "On Power: A Discussion of Richard Rorty and Michel Foucault." *World Communication* 25: 13–20.

———. 1997. *Conducting Socially Responsible Research: Critical Theory, Neo-Pragmatism, and Rhetorical Inquiry*. Thousand Oaks: Sage.

Tonkinson, Carole, ed. 1995. *Big Sky Mind: Buddhism and the Beat Generation*. New York: Riverhead.

Turner, Victor. 1967. *The Forest of Symbols: Aspects of Ndembu Ritual*. Ithaca: Cornell University Press.

———. 1969. *The Ritual Process: Structure and Anti-Structure*. Chicago: Aldine.

Tytell, John. 1976. *Naked Angels: The Lives and Literature of the Beat Generation*. New York: McGraw-Hill.

Vincinus, Martha. 1982. "Sexuality and Power: A Review of Current Work in the History of Sexuality." *Feminist Studies* 8: 133–56.

Viorst, Milton. 1979. *Fire in the Streets: America in the 1960s*. New York: Simon and Schuster.

Walker, Jeanne Murry. 1987. "Totalitarian and Liminal Societies in Zamyatin's *We*." *Mosaic* 20: 114–27.

Walker, Samuel. 1980. *Popular Justice: A History of American Criminal Justice*. Oxford: Oxford University Press.

Watts, Allen. 1958. "Beat Zen, Square Zen, and Zen." *Chicago Review* 12: 3–11.

Weaver, Richard M. 1948. *Ideas Have Consequences*. Chicago: University of Chicago Press.

White, Hayden. 1987. *The Content of the Form*. Baltimore: Johns Hopkins University Press.

Whorf, Benjamin Lee. 1956. *Language, Thought, and Reality*. Cambridge, MA: MIT Press.

Whyte, William Hollingsworth. 1956. *The Organization Man*. New York: Simon and Schuster.

Will, George F. 1988. "Daddy, Who Was Kerouac?" *Newsweek*, 4 July, 64.

Williams, Charles E. 1987. "Fantasy Theme Analysis: Theory vs. Practice." *Rhetoric Society Quarterly* 17: 11–20.

Williams, William Carlos. 1946. *Paterson*. New York: New Directions.

Wilson, Sloan. 1955. *The Man in the Gray Flannel Suit*. New York: Simon and Schuster.

Wolfe, Tom. 1968. *The Electric Kool-Aid Acid Test*. New York: Farrar, Straus, and Giroux.

Zandt, James E. Van. 1958. Loyalty Day 1958. *Congressional Record* 104. Proceedings and Debates of the 85th Congress, Second Session. Washington: United States Government Printing Office. 8181–82.

Index

African Americans (*see also* racism): portrayal of in *On the Road,* 86–89
agitation (*see also* deviance, lateral; deviance, vertical), 64, 67–69, 70–73
Alberts, J. K., 41
America (*see also* culture, American): as subject of *On the Road,* 83
amplification, 43–44, 75
Anctil, Pierre, 25
art, 39–42
autobiography, 3, 4, 61

Backman, Mark, 46
Bales, Robert F., 54; on fantasy themes and group behavior, 13–14, 43–44, 45, 51
Baraka, Amiri, 5, 20
Barthes, Roland, 68
Beat Generation (*see also* Kerouac, Jack; *On the Road*), 5, 9, 16, 24–26, 31, 82; liminality and, 99; and the meaning of Beat, 11–12; spirituality of, 92–93
behaviors, group, 46; Bales on, 13–14, 43–44, 45, 51
Berry, Mary Francis, 88
Bettencourt, Rita (*On the Road*), 78–79
Bhabba, Homi K., 86
Bible. *See* Christianity

Bird, William, 64
Black, Edwin: critique of fantasy theme analysis by, 52–53
Blackstock, Nelson, 28
Blassingame, John, 88
bohemianism, 107n. 12
bop: significance of, for Kerouac, 9–10, 11
Bormann, Ernest G., 26, 73, 84, 92–93; on fantasy theme analysis, 54, 55–56; and Hart's critique of fantasy theme analysis, 48–50; and innovation dramas, 85, 86; Mohrmann's critique of, 50–52; on rhetorical visions, 7–8
Bowers, John Waite: on agitation, 67–69, 70; and fantasy theme analysis, 57–58
Bridges, Bill, 73
Brock, Bernard L.: on symbolic convergence theory, 47–48
Buchanan, Richard: on amplification, 43–44
Bull (*On the Road*), 71–72
bums (*see also* poverty), 21–22
Burke, Kenneth, 4, 6, 8, 26, 35, 45; on art, 39–41; on consubstantiality, 84; on logology, 73; on piety, 12–13, 105–6n. 6; on style, 10
Burroughs, William S., 5, 6, 15, 16, 71

Index

Index

Index

Omar Swartz earned his Ph.D. in communication in 1995 from Purdue University. He is the author of *Conducting Socially Responsible Research: Critical Theory, Neo-Pragmatism, and Rhetorical Inquiry* and *The Rise of Rhetoric and Its Intersections with Modern Critical Thought*. He is currently a law student at Duke University.

DATE DUE